Nuclear Weapons:
The Last Great Debate?

Nuclear Weapons:
The Last Great Debate?

Peter Griffiths

Edward Arnold

© Peter Griffiths 1987

First published in Great Britain 1987 by
Edward Arnold (Publishers) Ltd, 41 Bedford Square, London WC1B 3DQ

Edward Arnold (Australia) Pty Ltd, 80 Waverley Road, Caulfield East, Victoria 3145, Australia

British Library Cataloguing in Publication Data
  Griffiths, Peter, *1939–*
  Nuclear weapons : the last great debate?
  1. Nuclear weapons
  I. Title
  358'.39   U264

ISBN 0-7137-7492-7

This book is for my wife, Maureen,
and my children, Kathryn and Matthew

Grateful thanks to Janet Stills for
typing the manuscript.

Text set in 10/12 pt CRTronic 300 Univers by Anneset, Weston-super-Mare, Avon
Printed and bound by The Bath Press, Bath, Avon

Contents

Preface

The thought that every one of us could be killed in one swift action used to be something read about in science fiction or watched on cinema screens; it was something in a world of make-believe inhabited by power-crazed dictators and mindless robots.

Now, the threat of total destruction by nuclear explosion is very real indeed.

How has this situation come about? Can anything be done to change it? It is the purpose of this book to try to answer these and other questions.

A great deal of emphasis in the book is placed on the United States; this does not show a bias for or against the Americans, but simply reflects the fact that information from American sources is readily available. 'Hard' facts from Russian sources are not easy to obtain; Britain, also, does not readily offer much information; you can learn more about this country's nuclear weapons from American sources than from our own!

Some of the sections call for tasks to be carried out that involve 'role-playing'; which means you pretend to be someone else. Role-playing can be a useful tool for several reasons. Firstly, it helps you to understand a situation because its component parts have to be separated and each one assigned to a player. Secondly, it makes for a more thorough and thoughtful investigation because once a role is assigned you will seek to defend and identify with that role.

Remember, however, that role-playing can have certain limitations. For example, it does not accurately match the passage of time in 'real' situations. Bear in mind also that you will never play any role *perfectly,* and that you will tend to behave more recklessly than you would in a real situation.

Finally, always remember that role-playing is a game: it is *not real.*

Acknowledgements

The publishers would like to thank the following for their permission to reproduce copyright photographs and diagrams:

Cover photograph by Roger P. Adkin (with assistance from SLR Photography); Los Alamos National Laboratory: p 1; US Department of Energy: p 3; John Topham Picture Library: p 9; Popperfoto: pp 11, 15; National Air Survey Centre: p 14; Jules Feiffer © 1978: p 19; U.S. Air Force: pp 22, 73t (MSGT Don Sutherland), 74; U.S. Navy: p 25; Central Office of Information: p 32; Hamish Hamilton Ltd: from *When the Wind Blows,* Raymond Briggs: p 36; Steve Kelly: p 37; John Stuart Clark: pp 39, 53; Lurie: pp 51, 75b; United Nations: p 52 (John Isaac); Society for Cultural Relations with the USSR/The Elsie Timbey Collection: p 59; Ministry of Defence (Crown Copyright): pp 73m and b, 81, 84m and b; Richard Cobb: p. 76; Rentasnap/John Birdsall: p 83; Duncan Mil: p 85; The Observer: p 95; Peter Kennard: p 104.

Special thanks go to Duncan Campbell and Patrick Forbes of the *New Statesman* for their help in preparing and providing updated information and the photographs for the *Bunkers of Britain* diagram on page 106, and for updating the US Bases map as provided by Michael Joseph Ltd on page 89.

While every attempt has been made to trace the holders of the copyright material on pages 51, 75b and 76 this has not been possible. Edward Arnold offer their apologies to anyone to whom they have failed to give the correct acknowledgement.

1   A journey to a city that used to be

You were indoors when the hydrogen bomb exploded; it was a pleasant, spring day and you were fifty miles away. You had not noticed the blue-white flash of light which had, for an instant, turned the blue sky a deep, inky black.

When you went outside you saw the people blinded by the flash of light. Some of them would recover their sight, but others, who had been staring directly towards the bomb, had melting eyeballs. They were screaming.

You did not know what had happened to them; you had not experienced the first of the many devastating effects of a nuclear explosion.

When you set off for the city that morning you expected an uneventful journey. You met more blind people on the way, but it was only when you reached the suburbs of the city, nineteen miles away from its centre, that you realised something was seriously wrong. Nearly all the houses had their windows smashed or missing; the road was strewn with broken glass; roofs had slates or tiles missing; chimney stacks had tumbled down and lay, as heaps of rubble, in the road; some of the houses were on fire.

The people you met had nasty wounds on their faces caused by flying slivers of glass.

What had happened? A gas main explosion? A storm force wind?

A wall of heat followed by a wind of hurricane force had ripped through this area; but you did not know that; nor did you know that no matter from which direction you had come into the city that day, north, east, south or west, you would have found the same things.

As you went further down the road which led directly to the city centre conditions became worse. About fourteen miles out people, with burns on their faces and bodies, could be seen. They were not dead — yet.

You were nine miles from the centre when, possibly for the first time, you needed a really strong stomach and a lot of courage to go even a yard further. You should have turned back there and then; but you did not.

Exploding the bomb

The people who lay on the road in front of you were dead; their bodies blackened and charred beyond recognition. Most of the houses had completely lost their roofs; walls had collapsed, burying and crushing their inhabitants; the houses were on fire. The road in front of you was covered with rubble.

It was two miles further on that you met the wall of fire; everything that could burn was ablaze. If there were people alive you could not find them. The air was thick with near-choking smoke and fumes.

You went on through what remained of the city's suburbs. Four miles from the city centre the fires still raged and all the houses were smashed down. They did not look as if they had fallen down, but seemed to have been ripped from their foundations, lifted into the air and thrown down. A few of the better-built, tall inner-city tower blocks still stood, although they were badly damaged. Half the people who lived in this area were dead in what remained of their houses and flats, or out on the streets mangled and crushed by falling rubble. Gas, electricity and water mains were all destroyed; and still the fires raged on with a searing, scorching heat. If you had been walking through this area when the bomb exploded you would have been burned to the bone before a shrieking, howling wind picked you up and threw you into the air as if you had been the lightest feather in the world.

Three miles from the city centre it looked like someone driving a giant roadroller had gone mad; for here everything had gone. The damage was total. The area flattened completely. The offices, shops, the roads, the people all gone.

The heart of the city had been a busy commercial, shopping and entertainment area. All that was left of it now was a deep, deep hole in the ground. The hole stretched the length of ten football pitches. It was as if the ground had opened up and swallowed the city centre. It was no use looking down the hole to see if the centre of the city was lying down there; still as neatly arranged as it had been at ground level. The city centre was not down there; it was above your head. It had been smashed into tiny pieces and sucked into the sky by the howling, roaring fireball of heat at the centre of the exploding hydrogen bomb.

As you stood and stared the city centre did start to come back to earth, but not as bricks or concrete or glass, but as flakes of ash; some light, some dark. It looked like a two-toned snowfall. Some of the flakes landed on you.

And from that moment on you started to die.

You turned away from the crater that had once been a city centre and made your way, as best you could, through the remains of the burning and shattered city to your home.

When you got back you felt very tired; so tired that all you wanted to do was to lie down and go into a long, deep sleep. But you could not rest because suddenly you felt very ill, so ill, you had to be sick; over and over again. You had attacks of diarrhoea and blood began to seep out of your gums into your mouth and over your lips. Your hair, lifeless, fell from your head in large clumps.

You had radiation sickness.

The falling flakes at the crater's edge were packed with deadly radiation. You had survived all the horrors of travelling through the effects of a nuclear explosion. You had not been blinded by the light-flash, burned or charred by the heat, deafened, smashed or buried by the blast wave; but the radioactive fallout, lingering above the city, had chosen its moment and fallen down on you.

After a few days of agony a sort of miracle happened. You started to feel better. The pain left you. You began to eat and drink again; you even sat up and took notice of the world around you. You had recovered from radiation sickness.

You did not know, nor really ever knew,

that deep inside the marrow of your bones the radioactive poison was still there; the damage was too severe for you to fully recover. You had shaken off the first effects, but a few weeks later they returned and this time you did not get over them.

You died.

[Based on effects of a single 5 megaton explosion at ground level.]

1

2

3

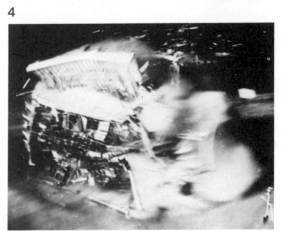

4

The effect of a nuclear explosion on a house

2 What happens when a nuclear weapon explodes

When a nuclear weapon explodes many things happen in a very short space of time:

● a brilliant blue-white **light flash** is accompanied by a huge explosion

● a **fireball**, nearly as hot as the centre of the Sun, is formed and shoots upwards and outwards

● the **heat** waves from the fireball race away from the centre of the explosion causing burns and fires

● then comes a shock wave, its enormously strong winds destroying buildings and people in its path; this shock wave is called **blast**; although you cannot see it, it is rather like running at full speed into a brick wall.

A nuclear explosion also releases what is called **prompt** or **initial radiation** in the form of deadly neutrons and gamma rays. The area covered by this prompt radiation, particularly in the larger **yield** nuclear weapons, is also covered by the effects of

EFFECTS OF A SINGLE NUCLEAR EXPLOSION
(all distances in miles from groundzero)

BLAST ZONES	WEAPON YIELD		WEAPON YIELD	
	1 MEGATON		5 MEGATONS	
	AIRBURST	GROUNDBURST	AIRBURST	GROUNDBURST
TOTAL DESTRUCTION	2¾	2	4¾	3¼
DAMAGE WHICH CANNOT BE REPAIRED	4⅓	2¾	7½	4¾
SEVERE DAMAGE	9½	5¾	16½	9¾
SOME DAMAGE	14+	8¾	30+	18¾
CRATER AT CENTRE OF EXPLOSION: RADIUS IN YARDS	—	710	—	1100
HEAT EFFECTS ON SKIN: VERY SERIOUS/CHARRING	9	5	16	9
BURNS NEEDING MEDICAL ATTENTION	12	8	20	14

Sources: US Office of Technology Assessment, *The Effects of Nuclear War,* Croom Helm, 1980. S. Glasstone and P. J. Dolan, *The Effects of Nuclear Weapons,* US Department of Defense, 1977. Home Office, *Nuclear Weapons,* HMSO, 1980.

Note: Nuclear weapons can be exploded in the air, on or near the ground, underground or underwater. The table above gives you the different ranges of damage caused by a **groundburst** and an **airburst** weapon.

the heat and blast waves.

The table on page 4 gives the details of the heat and blast damage caused by a single nuclear explosion.

The table below gives the effects of **blast damage** on people and property from a *single groundburst 5 megaton weapon*; distances in miles. Figures and effects are derived from the same sources as the previous table.

Groundzero to 3¼ miles

People	:	98% dead; 2% injured.
Property	:	most buildings destroyed.
Wind Speed	:	330 mph at time of explosion.

3¼ miles to 4¾ miles

People	:	50% dead; 40% injured.
Property	:	houses destroyed; severe damage to high-rise or tower buildings.
Wind Speed	:	165–330 mph.

4¾ miles to 9¾ miles

People	:	5% dead; 45% injured.
Property	:	severe damage to houses.
Wind Speed	:	70–165 mph.

9¾ miles to 18¾ miles

People	:	none dead; 25% injured.
Property	:	some damage; windows, tiles, doors blown out or off.
Wind Speed	:	35–70 mph.

Note: The light flash from the explosion can travel many miles (over 100), causing varying degrees of eye-damage.

The Terms Used: What They Mean

Airburst Nuclear Weapon: weapon exploded in the atmosphere below 100 000 feet.

Gamma Rays: a very penetrating form of electromagnetic radiation.

Groundburst Nuclear Weapon: weapon exploded on or immediately above the ground.

Groundzero: point on the ground at or immediately beneath the centre of a nuclear explosion.

Megaton: the explosive power of nuclear weapons is always expressed in either *kilotons* or *megatons*. As we shall see later, atomic bombs are measured in kilotons and hydrogen bombs in megatons. *Kilo* means one thousand; *mega* means one million. Nuclear weapons are measured as equivalent to the power of an ordinary or conventional explosive called TNT (trinitro-toluene); so kiloton is equivalent to 1 000 tons of TNT and 1 megaton is equivalent to 1 000 000 tons of TNT. The biggest bomb exploded during World War II used 10 tons of TNT.

Neutron: a particle from the centre or nucleus of an atom with effects similar to gamma rays.

Prompt or **Initial Radiation**: neutrons and gamma rays given out by nuclear weapons at the time of an explosion.

Yield: the explosive power of a nuclear weapon in kilotons (KTS) or megatons (MTS).

Another effect of a nuclear explosion is a brief surge of electro-magnetic energy sometimes called a 'radio flash', or more properly an **electromagnetic pulse (EMP)**. When a nuclear weapon was exploded high above the Pacific Island of Johnstone in 1958 the street lights in Hawaii, 625 miles away failed. EMP had caused this.

EMP destroys computer systems, telephone networks, any radio using an aerial and television sets which are switched on. EMP would spread many miles from the centre of a nuclear explosion over whole continents. In wartime the major effects of EMP would be the disruption of military command and control systems and civil defence warning systems.

Why Nuclear Weapons Are Not Just Big Bangs

The destructive power of one nuclear weapon can equal hundreds or thousands of ordinary or conventional bombs. This is enough to make them different, but what makes them so very different is **radioactive fallout**.

Radioactive fallout occurs when a nuclear weapon is exploded on or near the ground because the explosion causes huge amounts of earth to be sucked up into the air. Particles of the earth become contaminated by radiation from the explosion and then return to the ground.

Most fallout comes down close to where a bomb has exploded and dies away very quickly. It is claimed that you would be safe from the worst effects of radioactive fallout some two weeks after a nuclear explosion.

For those badly affected by radiation the end would come within a few hours, days or weeks after bouts of vomiting, diarrhoea, bleeding from the mouth and bowels, hair loss and fever had brought about heart failure or the total breakdown of the nervous system.

Those who survive the first fallout from a bomb cannot be sure that they will not eventually die from blood diseases or cancer months or years later. People who suffered from radiation during the atomic bomb explosions on the Japanese cities of Hiroshima and Nagasaki are still dying from its effects over thirty-five years later.

Some radioactive particles are thrown high into the sky after an explosion and these, caught up by the winds in the upper atmosphere, may travel many miles away to contaminate areas that neither saw the light flash from the bomb nor heard the deafening bang of the explosion.

The map that follows shows the possible fallout effect from a single explosion.

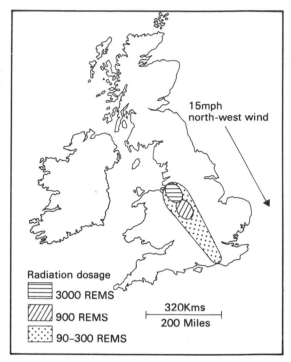

Radioactive fallout 'blanket' from one groundburst 1 megaton hydrogen bomb, superimposed on a map of England

Note: Amounts of radiation can be measured in either **rads** or **rems**. The difference between them is that a rad only tells you how much is taken in by a living organism, it does not tell you how much of that radiation is damaging. For this aspect of radiation the other measure — the rem — is used; it can measure the amount of radiation that *actually harms* living things.

If you receive 900 rems or more you will die within days. More than 300 rems could cause death, radiation sickness or delayed cancer.

The danger from radioactive fallout does not stop with mere distance travelled. Some radioactive particles can last a very long time and continue to affect people and the earth for hundreds or thousands of years.

Radioactive particles such as Strontium 90, Caesium 137 and Carbon 14 last a very long time. Carbon 14 has a half-life of 5730 years. A half-life is the time needed for one half of a given amount of a radioactive element to decay.

These poisons would enter our bodies through the things we eat and drink causing cancers and, it is claimed, genetic malformations, which means that children could be born with physical abnormalities.

If a nuclear weapon destroyed a nuclear power station or a nuclear fuel processing plant then the radioactive fallout would be more serious than that from a single bomb. The nuclear plant at Sellafield, which used to be called Windscale, processes waste from many nuclear power stations. The map that follows shows what could happen to Britain if it was destroyed.

Radioactive fallout 'blanket' resulting from destruction of nuclear plant at Sellafield assuming north-west wind blowing

We have seen the possible effects of radioactive fallout from a single nuclear bomb and from the destruction of Sellafield. Nobody can be sure that these things are completely accurate; radioactive fallout patterns are very difficult to predict as they depend on so many different factors such as weapon yield, wind speed and direction and weather conditions. However, the effects of radioactivity in an all-out nuclear war would be catastrophic.

TASKS: Chapters 1 and 2

1. Obtain a map of your local area and using the information given in the table on page 4 draw the blast and heat effects from:
   a) an airburst weapon, and
   b) a groundburst weapon.
   Decide where the centre of the explosion is and draw circles outwards from that.

2. Take time to travel around your local area and note what will have gone after the nuclear explosion. Remember that your results do not take into account the effects of radioactive fallout.

3. Compare the map on page 6 with a map of Britain that shows the towns and cities and see which of them would be affected. Remember that this is the effect of a single nuclear explosion; in a war there would be many more radioactive plumes.

4. The map on this page shows the possible radioactive fallout blanket from the destruction of the nuclear processing plant at Sellafield (Windscale). The map also gives the locations of some of Britain's nuclear power stations. What areas could be affected if any or all of these were destroyed by a nuclear weapon? Remember that wind direction can alter the area covered with fallout.

3 All-out nuclear war

The world's arsenals contain tens of thousands of nuclear weapons, probably as many as 60 000. The total explosive power of these weapons is equivalent to . . . about 4 tons of TNT for every man, woman and child on earth. If all, or a significant proportion of them, were used, the consequences would be beyond imagination.
(F. Barnaby, *Prospects For Peace,* Pergamon International Library, 1980.)

A new world war can hardly fail to involve the all-out use of nuclear weapons. Such a war would not drag on for years. It could be all over in a matter of days. And when it is all over what will the world be like? Our fine great buildings, our homes will exist no more. The thousands of years it took to develop our civilisation will have been in vain. Our works of art will be lost. Radio, television, newspapers will disappear. There will be no hospitals. No help can be expected for the few mutilated survivors in any town to be sent from a neighbouring town — there will be no neighbouring town left, no neighbours, there will be no help, there will be no hope.
(Lord Louis Mountbatten, 11 May 1979, Strasbourg.)

Every weapon invented has been tested in battle; military people could see clearly the effects of advances in weaponry.

The long-bow used by Henry V's Welsh archers at the Battle of Agincourt showed the helplessness of the heavily armoured rider. The use of tanks by the Germans in World War II revolutionised ideas of how future wars could be fought. Throughout history there have been many changes and a great deal of progression in the use of weapons.

The only weapon never tested in battle conditions is the nuclear weapon. The effects of a single nuclear weapon are known, but what would happen if a great many nuclear weapons were used in an all-out war? It would be right to say that it would be the greatest disaster ever inflicted on people; it could be the end of civilisation as we know it.

Some people say that a war could be fought using only a limited number of nuclear weapons. This could be the case, but we know from the plans of the nuclear countries that a great many weapons would be used.

We must assume the worst.

The Effects of All-out Nuclear War

The 'Doomsday Machine' was never built; but it was suggested in the United States in the 1950s. If the Russians attacked the United States they could never hope to win; the Doomsday Machine would see to that.

The idea was to bury a great many hydrogen bombs deep in the earth's crust throughout the United States. When the Russians attacked, the bombs would be exploded, destroying the earth's crust and taking the Americans, the Russians and the rest of us with it.

The thought of the earth's crust crumbling beneath us is one example of the more extreme effects of the explosion of thousands of bombs in an all-out nuclear war. Others include the suggestion that the force generated by all these explosions would knock the earth out of orbit and send it hurtling across space to be consumed by the fires of the sun; or that the heat from the explosions would cause the oxygen in the earth's atmosphere to burn up and extinguish all life on earth.

These are extreme ideas, or so it is said. We have never had a nuclear war to see if they are right and if they were, then there may be nobody left alive to say, 'told you so'.

An allied correspondent looks down on the remains of a Japanese barber shop in devastated Hiroshima

Most scientists do agree, however, that certain things would be likely to happen all over the world; even though the main force of a nuclear attack would fall on America, the Soviet Union and Europe. Millions would die — instantly; millions more would eventually die from the effects of radioactive fallout.

High up in the atmosphere is the ozone layer; it protects us from the full effects of the heat of the sun. All-out nuclear war could break up the ozone layer. The intense heat would then penetrate the earth, burning and blinding people, animals and insects and destroying crops in the ground. What would life be like for any survivors?

The World Has Turned Inside Out

You went to bed last night; the light worked; the gas flowed; water still dripped from the tap in the kitchen that should have been mended long ago; all was quiet; the roads empty.

You had a nightmare; somewhere in the night fires were burning, buildings had collapsed. The light beside your bed did not work; the tap had stopped dripping, its water dried up. The radio and television were dead. You felt frightened and alone.

The first sign that your nightmare was not just a bad dream, but reality, was the faint rumble of distant traffic; heavy traffic; lots of it, coming from the north where the big town was.

You went to the window and stared at them as they came down your road. They were packed into cars and lorries and some in buses. Anything that would move seemed to be moving. It was, at first glance, like a great trip to the seaside until you saw their faces. This was no seaside trip; these were refugees fleeing the destruction of their town; some in panic; some in shock; all in desperation.

The Refugees

Any survivors of a nuclear attack might try to escape the scene of destruction. The roads would be jammed. There would be no emergency centres ready to receive them. The available food would only be sufficient for the needs of the local people, not the great hordes from the town. Probably there would be trouble for the refugees would be hungry and thirsty.

How would they be dealt with? In Britain as follows:

> In conditions in which death, destruction and injury were commonplace, such penalties as probation, fines or sentences of imprisonment would no longer be effective . . . in the case of flagrantly anti-social behaviour there might be a need for harsher penalties than would be generally acceptable in peacetime . . .
> (Home Office Emergency Services Circular E3/1976.)

The Injured

The refugees could move about but behind them they left the badly injured. In normal times badly injured people receive full medical treatment; times are no longer normal; all-out nuclear war has happened.

This is to be the fate of these people:

> . . . After a nuclear attack, radioactive fallout, either in the area or drifting towards it, might be at lethal or near lethal levels. It would be essential that [Health Service] staff, vital to the long-term recovery of the country, should not be wasted by allowing them to enter areas of high radioactivity and no staff should leave shelter until authorised to do so . . .
> (Home Office Emergency Services Circular ES1/1977.)

The Corpses and Disease

Millions of dead bodies would lie among the ruins; it would be almost impossible to clear them; they would not receive a proper burial.

Rotting corpses, the destruction of the water supply and sewerage systems would lay the seeds for outbreaks of diseases such as tetanus, typhus, tuberculosis, dysentery, diphtheria and possibly bubonic plague. There would be few vaccines to deal with the situation and perhaps even fewer doctors and nurses left alive. The medical services would be overwhelmed.

The Able-Bodied Survivors

Their minds would be filled with the horrors they had seen — the fires, the hideously wounded, the deaths of friends and family. Some would be in a state of deep shock; some angry and violent; others would commit suicide. Everything they had known would be gone or changed so completely as to no longer have any meaning.

They would soon be hungry and desperately thirsty; those who could think ahead would know that the air above and around them was filled with a lethal rain of radioactive fallout. The instinct to survive is one of the human race's strongest drives; some of the able-bodied might survive foraging for food in the radioactive desert that was once their world; but everything would be against them and soon after the last nuclear explosion the nuclear winter would descend on them.

The Nuclear Winter

The dust and smoke from fires caused by relatively few nuclear explosions would bring about an unbroken darkness over the whole northern hemisphere and might spread to the southern hemisphere and cover the entire world.

There would be a rapid and dramatic drop in temperature caused by the darkness which would last for several months. The temperature would sink below freezing in

10

A nuclear desert

this permanent night. Plant growth would be halved or severely limited; animals would die of thirst because water supplies would be frozen. Human beings would starve to death.

Tropical forests would suffer badly as they cannot stand cold and dark conditions even for short periods; they could disappear altogether.

Fires in urban areas would cause large amounts of poisonous fumes from the burning of synthetic materials to be let off.

The idea of the nuclear winter was first brought to public notice by a conference of scientists held in Washington DC in October and November 1983. All the information available since then has confirmed the original findings about the scope and intensity of the nuclear winter.

> One must conclude that a full-scale nuclear holocaust could lead to the extinction of mankind.
> (J. Schell, *The Fate of the Earth*, Picador, 1982.)

> There is a terrible phrase in our documents 'the living will envy the dead'. But it is true.
> (Dr Evgeni Chazov, *New Scientist*, 8/10/81.)

TASKS: Chapter 3

1. Read the Home Office circular E3/1976 on page 10. Explain what you think it means.

2. Look at the Home Office circular ES1/1977 on page 10. If you were a doctor or nurse would you follow this order? Give your reasons.

3. You are a member of your local civil defence committee; it is your job to help plan for any emergencies that result from a nuclear war.

    The Government has told the committee that it cannot expect any immediate help from outside.

    One of the problems after a nuclear attack could be what to do about refugees coming into your area. You must expect that any refugees would be hungry, thirsty and desperate.

    Your committee is about to hold a meeting on the subject of refugees. The committee has representatives from the police, the military, the health authority and local government officials.

    A number of suggestions are put forward at the meeting.
    a) refugees should be rounded up and isolated in temporary camps;
    b) they should be escorted or forced out of the area;
    c) attempts should be made to feed and house all of them; and
    d) they could be divided into categories of medical need and dealt with according to these.

    What do you think could be the consequences of each of these actions? Which one do you favour? And why?

    Is there any other course of action you would follow that is not on the list? What could be the consequences of this?

    Remember when answering you must bear in mind: (a) your local resources of food, shelter and medical supplies are limited; and (b) help from outside may be a *very long time* in coming.

4. Although your local area has survived; a nuclear attack has destroyed all its *mains* water, gas and electricity

supplies. The radio, television and telephone services are dead. No help can be expected from neighbouring districts. You are in your home with your family. You can travel only up to two miles, in any direction. After this, movement is impossible.

In addition to your home, which provides shelter, here is a list of basic essentials for survival: water, warmth and food.

Keep these in mind and try to answer these questions about your *immediate* survival.

How much drinking water is there in your home? Remember that some foods contain water.

Is there a supply of drinkable water within two miles of your home? (Water is the first essential for human survival — after two days without moisture intake most people will die. People can last about sixty days without food.)

How will you keep warm?

How much food have you got? How will you cook it? How long will it last?

You might supplement your food by eating animals and plants.

Are there any animals in your district which could be killed and eaten?

Do you know which plants are safe to eat?

How will you know if any plants and water are not contaminated by radio-active fallout?

Do you think you will even care by then?

5. You are in charge of your local area after a nuclear attack; you do not have enough supplies to last for very long; no help can be expected from outside. You have to choose who will be given supplies and who will not. How would you go about this? And how would you make everyone accept your decisions?

4   How nuclear weapons came into our world

Adolf Hitler knew what he wanted; he would stop at nothing to achieve his aims. Both in words and actions Hitler made it plain that the future was to be a German future. The German 'Master Race' would control the European continent; all other nations, with a few exceptions, were to be reduced to slavery and some were to be exterminated.

Hitler's armies, using the most advanced military technology, had, in two years, overrun most of Europe. By the autumn of 1941 his forces were converging on Moscow to deal the final blow to his Russian enemies.

Britain, although undefeated, stood alone and incapable of stopping Hitler. He was so confident of his success that he declared war on the United States only four days after the Japanese had attacked and destroyed most of the American Pacific Fleet at Pearl Harbor on 7 December 1941.

The year 1942 saw the seemingly unstoppable advance of the German and Japanese war machines. For the United States the situation was very serious and the future darker still. The Japanese and Germans were succeeding in isolating the American continent from the rest of the world. The world's major industrial and population centres were falling to them. It did not seem likely that the Germans and Japanese would extend the hand of friendship to America once they had finished their conquests. It was more probable that America would be their next target.

Advances in military technology, par-ticularly in submarine warfare and long-range bombers would sooner or later bring the United States within attacking distance of the Japanese and Germans.

It was not only the speed of technical advances that worried America but, more importantly, the type of advances. The Germans were developing a uranium or atomic bomb; a weapon rumoured to be able to destroy a whole town with one explosion. Hitler, armed with this new bomb and aircraft capable of reaching the United States, was a terrifying threat. Scientists in America were only too well aware of the danger:

> We must have some countermeasure available to meet any possible threat to atomic warfare by Germany.
> (R. Jungk, *Brighter Than 1000 Suns,* Penguin, 1960.)

Advances in nuclear physics (the study of atoms, the smallest particles of matter), had shown that it was possible to make an atomic bomb. In 1939, French scientists had discovered that a **nuclear chain reaction** was possible and a year before this the discovery had been made that atoms of uranium could be made to split or **fission** and so release enormous amounts of energy. This discovery was made in Nazi Germany.

Together these two pieces of knowledge meant that a bomb of massive destructive power could be built.

Albert Einstein, the most famous nuclear physicist of his time, wrote a letter to the American President, Franklin Roosevelt pointing out the dangers of a German atomic bomb. The result of Einstein's efforts was to change world history through the Manhattan Project.

The project was hurried, expensive and highly secret; carried out in the United States it employed nearly 40 000 people at thirty-seven installations and its aim was to make an atomic bomb before Hitler did.

Much work had already been done in America on nuclear fission under the leadership of a scientist called Enrico Fermi. It was Fermi's team which, in December 1942, produced the world's first **controlled nuclear chain reaction**. Without this work the development of the atomic bomb might have been slowed down considerably. The push behind the American effort was summed up by Dr Crawford Greenwalt, a scientist working with Fermi:

> We all had this great fear that the Nazis would make the discovery before we did. I used to come downstairs in the mornings afraid to pick up the newspapers in case I would read that they had invented the bomb.
> (The *Observer,* 5/12/82.)

After Fermi's success in laying the groundwork for what is today the process used in nuclear power stations, the scientists turned their efforts to producing an atomic bomb under the leadership of Robert Oppenheimer, at Los Alamos, New Mexico.

Hitler did not make the first atomic bomb; the United States did. The first test explosion took place in July 1945 at Almogordo, New Mexico. The Germans had surrendered two months earlier. The scientists had done their work; they had done all that had been expected of them; now it was the turn of the politicians.

Harry S. Truman, President of the United States and Commander-in-Chief of the Armed Forces, could have ordered the close down of the Manhattan Project; the reason for it no longer existed. Germany had been beaten. But this was not to happen; Japan was still at war with America.

Truman had been told by his advisers that the war against Japan could drag on until at least November 1947. It would involve an invasion of Japan; one million American dead could be the result against a fanatical enemy for whom surrender in battle was the greatest shame, the worst of all humiliations. Despite the knowledge that the Japanese were not developing an atomic bomb and had already put out secret peace-feelers to the United States, Truman decided to go ahead and use the atomic bomb against Japan.

At 8.16 a.m. on 6 August 1945, an atomic bomb exploded above the Japanese city of Hiroshima; 140 000 people died. Three days later another atomic bomb was dropped and obliterated Nagasaki.

Japan surrendered. A Japanese journalist described the Hiroshima bomb:

> Suddenly a glaring ... light appeared in the sky accompanied by an unnatural tremor which was followed almost immediately by a wave of suffocating heat and a wind which swept away everything in its path. Within a few seconds the thousands of people in the streets in the centre of the town were scorched by a wave of searing heat. Many were killed instantly, others lay writhing on the ground screaming in agony from the intolerable pain of their burns. Everything standing upright in the way of the blast — walls, houses, factories and other buildings was annihilated ... Hiroshima had ceased to exist.
> (quoted by Lord Louis Mountbatten, 11 May 1979, Strasbourg.)

The Hiroshima 'little boy' atomic bomb

Sometimes the things we do have effects which do not hit us until days or months or years later; and so it was with the bombs that killed so many Japanese in August 1945. Very few people, outside Japan, understood the full implications of the discovery of nuclear weapons. In 1945 the atomic bomb was seen by most people as something which brought a speedy end to World War II. The number of people killed in Japan did not shock or horrify a world used to a daily diet of civilian deaths. The frightful destruction of British and German cities, for example, during World War II killed many more people.

The full consequences of nuclear weapons did not start to work through to most people until the 1950s and by then the nuclear age was well on its way to the 1980s.

The scientists' view was summed up by Einstein when he said: 'If only I had known I should have become a watchmaker.'

'Survivors' of Hiroshima

The Atomic Bomb is Joined by the Hydrogen Bomb September 1949: Washington, DC, capital city of the United States of America

Intelligence reaching Washington con-firmed that the Soviet Union had success-fully exploded its first atomic bomb.

By 1949 the relationship between the United States and the Soviet Union had become very strained; so much so that it was described as the Cold War. Their rivalry, mistrust, and dislike has fuelled the nuclear arms race down to the present day. Neither side has wanted or dared let the other get one step ahead.

In 1950, as a direct result of the Russian test explosion, the Americans went on to develop the 'superbomb' or hydrogen bomb. The principles for building such a bomb had been known since 1942. The hydrogen bomb is many times more powerful than the atomic bomb.

In November 1952 the Americans tested the first hydrogen bomb.

In August 1953 the Russians exploded their first hydrogen bomb.

In August 1954 the Americans tested a new, improved version of the hydrogen bomb.

And so the arms race was well underway; it continues today.

It has now been 35 years since the first atomic bomb fell on Hiroshima. The great majority of the world's people cannot remember a time when the nuclear shadow did not hang over the earth. Our minds have adjusted to it, as after a time our eyes adjust to the dark . . .

In an all-out nuclear war, more destructive power than in all of World War II would be unleashed every second for the long afternoon it would take for all missiles and bombs to fall. A World War II every second. . . more people killed in the first few hours than all wars of history put together. The survivors, if any, would live in despair, amid the poisoned ruins of a civilisation that had committed suicide.

(US President Carter, 15 January 1981.)

On the assumption that a Third World War must escalate to nuclear destruction I can tell you what the Fourth World War will be fought with — bows and arrows.

(Albert Einstein.)

15

The Processes Explained

1. *Fission*

When an atom of uranium or plutonium is bombarded by a subatomic particle called a neutron three things happen (see diagram below):

a) great amounts of heat energy are released; this is the reason for the formidable power of nuclear fission weapons;

b) two or more neutrons are released; and

c) two or more smaller atoms are released which are highly radioactive and give rise to prompt or initial radiation and eventually radioactive fallout.

Atoms which split in this way are called **fissile.**

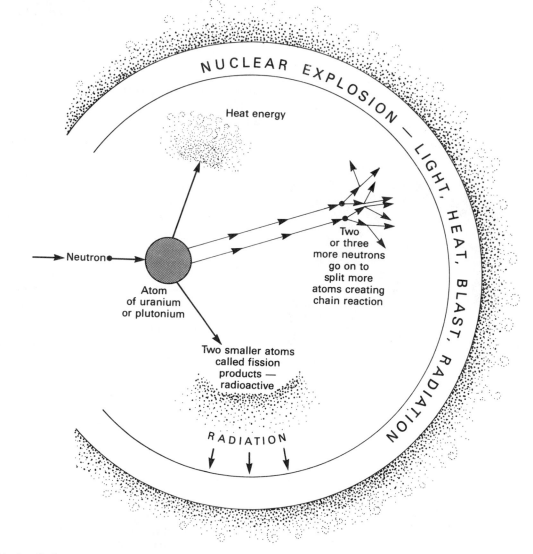

Nuclear fission process

2. *Nuclear chain reaction*

The neutrons given off when an atom splits go on to hit other atoms causing them to split and so a chain reaction is created which involves billions of atoms and an enormous explosion. A **controlled** chain reaction involves slowing down a chain reaction so that heat is created which does not lead to an explosion. Controlled chain reactions are used in nuclear power stations.

TASKS: Chapter 4

1. Suppose you are president of a large, powerful country at war with another country that will inflict enormous casualties on your soldiers; you get nuclear weapons; you know you can save your soldiers if you use the weapons, but you also know that when you use them the world will enter a time when all human life can be destroyed. What do you do?

2. The scientists made them; the politicians ordered their use; the military obeyed that order. Who was most to blame? Remember that we today know far more about nuclear technology and its effects than was known in the 1940s and 1950s.

5   A word about words

The words people use when they talk about nuclear weapons are usually chosen very carefully. When you watch television or read newspapers notice the language that is used; sometimes it is difficult to appreciate that people are talking about the same thing. For example is an 'enhanced radiation device' the same as a 'neutron bomb'? The answer is yes!

Then why call the same thing by a different name? This depends on your point of view. If you want to persuade others that something which is essentially harmful and destructive is, in fact, not quite so bad as all that, you can go a long way towards this by making the object *sound* harmless.

A *device* sounds harmless; an enhanced radiation device could be a helpful kitchen utensil; perhaps it is part of a microwave oven. Whereas a neutron bomb does not sound in the least bit friendly or helpful; a bomb is a *bomb*; bombs maim and kill.

There are many other examples of word-changing when people talk about nuclear weapons. They serve as signs of the long-run and hard-fought argument between those who believe that nuclear weapons are the greatest evil ever invented and so must be removed from our world and those who think that these weapons are a fact of life and can neither be wished away nor the knowledge of them ever destroyed, and we must, therefore, live with them and, hopefully, control them.

Here are a few more examples of word-changing:

● *collateral damage* means the deaths of thousands of innocent people who happened to live close to a target struck by a nuclear weapon
● *nuclear deterrent* is a stockpile of thousands of atomic and hydrogen bombs ready for use against innocent civilians in a foreign country
● *acceptable loss* means the number of dead and injured a country thinks it can put up with and still go on functioning
● *European theatre weapons* are those bombs that would be used to devastate the towns, cities and countryside of Europe

Another danger associated with word-alteration is that the people who deal on a day-to-day basis with nuclear weapons will come to accept them as something other than they are; to see them in some way as objects of pride and devotion. Here is a description of the scene when a cruise missile was tested in the United States.

> As it went by the second time it dived and then soared again to *applause* from spectators . . . the helicopter with the missile slung beneath it then did a *lap of honour* over the small *delighted* crowd. Coffee and doughnuts were served by ladies from the Dugway Base High School. . . one missile a month will be selected at random from stocks deployed in Europe and tested to ensure the '*health*' [author's emphasis] of the missile stock.
> (The *Observer,* 8/4/84.)

This is not the description of a garden party or a local carnival, but a test flight of a missile with enough power in its warhead to utterly destroy a medium-sized town and all the people in it.

6 Nuclear weapons: how they work

The Atomic Bomb or Nuclear Fission Weapon

For our purposes we need to consider the behaviour of the atoms of two substances: Uranium 235 and Plutonium 239.

When U_{235} is bombarded by neutrons it splits and releases enormous amounts of energy. Pu_{239} has the same qualities as U_{235}. Atomic bombs use either U_{235} or Pu_{239} as their explosive force.

The atomic bomb is the cheapest, smallest, weapon of mass destruction the world has ever known.

The bomb dropped on Hiroshima contained 25 lbs of U_{235}; an amount which could be crammed inside a cricket or tennis ball.

It is difficult to imagine something as small as a cricket or tennis ball killing 140 000 people in Hiroshima; but it did.

The power or yield of an atomic bomb is measured as if it is equivalent to the power of TNT. The Hiroshima bomb had an explosive power of 12 500 tons of TNT, usually referred to as 12.5 kilotons (KTS). (Remember that a heavy air raid during World War II using hundreds of planes was usually around 3000 tons of TNT.)

However, the atomic bomb pales into insignificance beside the explosive power of the hydrogen bomb. The power of H-bombs is measured in megatons of TNT equivalent; remember that mega means million.

Such is the strength of hydrogen bombs that they use atomic bombs to trigger them off!

The Hydrogen Bomb or Thermonuclear Fusion Weapon

The high temperature created when an atomic bomb explodes is used to cause two varieties of hydrogen — deuterium or H^2 and tritium or H^3 — to come together or *fuse* to create another substance called helium. This fusion then causes the fission of Uranium $_{238}$.

U_{238} could not be used in the atomic bomb because it could not be made to split or fission. However, the enormously high temperatures created by the fusion process made this possible. U_{238} is much more plentiful and cheaper to make than U_{235}.

Although the hydrogen bomb should properly be called a 'uranium bomb' the name hydrogen bomb remains its usual name. It is the standard weapon fitted to most nuclear missiles and carried aboard aeroplanes.

Since the 1940s and 1950s there have been other developments in nuclear weaponry; for example the neutron bomb or enhanced radiation weapon and 'mini-nukes'.

The Neutron Bomb

This is a small-yield hydrogen bomb. Its special feature is that its output of heat and blast is much reduced and its output of deadly radiation is increased or enhanced. It is meant for use over small areas, perhaps only a few miles across, with the intention of killing people, but leaving property alone. The main use for the neutron bomb would be in Western Europe to kill Russian tank crews if they ever invaded and at the same time leave West German towns more or less untouched.

It is still, however, a nuclear weapon and the deaths it could cause would be great.

Mini-Nukes

Atomic bombs now exist that are very small in explosive power and size; the smallest is the American W54 atomic land-mine with a yield of 10 tons of TNT; the same as the largest bomb used in World War II. Mini-nukes can be fired by field guns as if they were ordinary shells.

Nowadays there is a nuclear bomb to fit almost any weapon, from 9MTS hydrogen bombs down to small atomic shells, depth charges and land-mines.

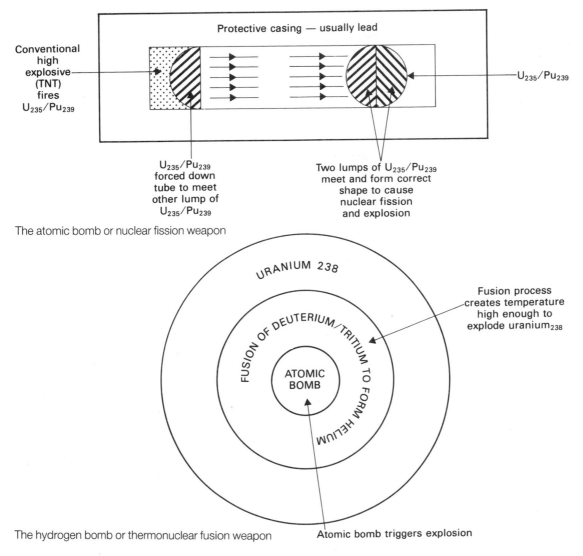

Protective casing — usually lead

Conventional high explosive (TNT) fires U_{235}/Pu_{239}

U_{235}/Pu_{239}

U_{235}/Pu_{239} forced down tube to meet other lump of U_{235}/Pu_{239}

Two lumps of U_{235}/Pu_{239} meet and form correct shape to cause nuclear fission and explosion

The atomic bomb or nuclear fission weapon

URANIUM 238

FUSION OF DEUTERIUM/TRITIUM TO FORM HELIUM

ATOMIC BOMB

Fusion process creates temperature high enough to explode uranium$_{238}$

The hydrogen bomb or thermonuclear fusion weapon

Atomic bomb triggers explosion

7 Nuclear delivery systems

The world has shrunk; not in size but in the time it takes to get from one place to another. Improvements in transport systems have made it possible to reach parts of the world in a matter of minutes or hours rather than days or weeks.

Nuclear weapon delivery systems have, along with other forms of transport, played a part in this shrinkage, although their cargoes are not people or goods, but deadly warheads.

A delivery system is a method of transporting a warhead from one place to another, from its launch pad to its target. There is little point in building an atomic or hydrogen bomb unless you have the means of getting it to its target; an effective delivery system is needed. People might feel alarmed if it was known that a country unfriendly to their own had got the 'bomb'. And rightly so; for every extra nuclear weapon is an additional threat to people's lives. However, the alarm bells would ring even louder if that country also possessed a delivery system effective enough to deliver the bomb.

Bombs are cheap; delivery systems are, on the whole, expensive. Many countries could produce nuclear weapons, but when it comes to delivery systems the United States and the Soviet Union dominate the world. These countries not only possess most nuclear weapons but also most of the world's delivery systems.

There are two forms of delivery system: aeroplanes and missiles.

The B-52 bomber

Aeroplanes

The aircraft that dropped the atomic bombs on Hiroshima and Nagasaki in August 1945 were piston-engined, propeller-driven American Superfortresses. In their day they were the most lethal delivery system ever invented, but nowadays they would appear as slow, lumbering beasts. Then in the mid-1950s the B52 arrived.

The jet-engined B52 (still in service) flying from bases dotted around the world was a major advance in delivery system technology. It was faster than the Superfortress, and it had a range which meant it could reach targets in Russia and return home again. Its major failing was time; it still took hours to reach its targets which gave Soviet air defences the chance to intercept and destroy it.

The Americans are now developing a new plane, the B1, which will fly faster than the speed of sound, carry more weapons than the B52 and more devices to confuse Russian air defence radar systems and so have a better chance of penetrating to its target areas. The latest development in the United States is the proposed 'Stealth' bomber which is being designed not to confuse Russian radar, but to evade it completely. Both these aircraft are expected to come into service during the 1990s.

The United States has many other aircraft in addition to its long-range bombers; these are called fighter-bombers or strike aircraft and are based in Europe or on aircraft carriers. They are nearly all capable of carrying nuclear bombs or short-range nuclear missiles.

The latest development for the American long-range bombers is the fitting of air-launched cruise missiles (ALCMs) beneath their wings which will give the Americans a powerful addition to an already formidable force.

The Russians do not have a plane capable of flying to the United States *and returning home*; an attack by plane on America would be a one-way journey for Russian pilots. However, the Russians do have a great many aircraft capable of attacking and returning after raids on Europe.

Missiles

There is no defence against missiles; with bombers there is a fighting chance of knocking them out of the sky, but hundreds or thousands of missile warheads would rain down certain death and destruction.

The missiles displaced the bomber as the main delivery system during the 1960s because they are faster and they certainly would reach their targets.

The Intercontinental Ballistic Missile (ICBM)

Both the United States and the Soviet Union have missiles capable of reaching each other's homelands in less than half-an-hour.

A ballistic missile is one that is aimed, fired into the earth's atmosphere and drops down on its target. As well as being quick most of today's ICBMs are also very accurate; they nearly always, when tested, fall where they are intended to fall. Some ICBMs are based on land either hidden in underground pits called silos or on mobile transporters which enable them to be carried from place to place.

The major problem with these land-based ICBMs is that the increased accuracy of missiles makes them vulnerable; vulnerable means capable of being harmed or destroyed. The fear among the military and politicians is that the other side could destroy them by striking first in a war. Both the Russians and the Americans have many vulnerable ICBMs; the problem is how to protect them from a surprise attack.

What can be done to save them?
What is your most precious possession? Find it; take it and stand it outside; pretend it is so heavy that you cannot move it about quickly.

You are approached by the world's most expert stonethrower. You know that if the stonethrower is in a bad mood or happens not to like you, your precious possession will be attacked and the stonethrower will not miss.

You must do something to protect your possession, but what? You cannot leave it where it is.

Plan A: Keep it moving; put it on wheels; even the world's best stonethrower might think twice about his chances of hitting a moving target.

Plan B: Do not simply keep it moving; but move it quickly up as many streets as possible and sometimes take it through an underground tunnel; double back on your tracks; keep the stonethrower confused as to its exact location.

Plan C: You know that the stonethrower's method of attack is to hurl stones rapidly one after the other; they would rain down on your precious possession very quickly. To protect against this put your possession inside a really hard cover and hope that when the first stone lands it does not damage the cover, but splinters into a thousand sharp pieces which fly out in all directions and knock out the other stones that have been thrown.

Military planners go to enormous lengths to try to protect land-based ICBMs. In the United States the latest proposed land-based missile, the MX, has gone through various suggestions which involve aspects of Plans A, B and C.

The first suggestions involved constructing mile upon mile of roadways along which MX would ride; the cost would have been huge. And the people who lived in the area where MX was to make its travels objected strongly; after all they realised that they would be prime targets for nuclear obliteration.

Plan C was later suggested. All the MX missiles were to be crammed together in a 'dense pack' fourteen miles by one mile. The first Soviet missiles to arrive and explode on the dense pack would create enough heat and blast to knock out all the others coming behind. This effect is known as fratricide (which means the murder of a brother or sister). This plan was abandoned because it was based on a highly unlikely and untested theory.

There were thirty-four different plans suggested for the siting of MX; some threatened to bankrupt the country or break international treaties or were based on untested ideas.

One of the main arguments against MX was that even if the Russians managed to knock out all the American land-based ICBMs and bombers this would still leave the United States with more than enough warheads to destroy the Soviet Union because over half of all US missile warheads are aboard submarines.

The Submarine Launched Ballistic Missile (SLBM)

No Russian submarine has ever managed to successfully track down and follow an American submarine.

While plans for land-based ICBMs involve almost incredible ideas to safeguard them, the weapons under the sea remain safe from attack. Operating at great depth in the immensity of the oceans of the world the nuclear submarine is, so far, safe from certain destruction. No matter how tempted an enemy might be to attack bombers and land-based ICBMs because their whereabouts can be pin-pointed the enemy would know that if this was done then a horrifying revenge would be visited on them from beneath the oceans.

Trident-launching nuclear submarine

Trident D5 which will make it possible by 1989 for submarines to strike targets 7 500 miles away. This is the missile that Britain is buying to replace Polaris.

MRV/MIRV/MARV

Bombs are cheap; missiles are expensive. Why waste an expensive missile by using only one warhead on it when you can put on lots of warheads; sometimes up to ten on each missile. The more warheads you place on a missile the more power you get; you can hit more targets and you can swamp any enemy defence system.

The first *MRVs (Multiple Re-entry Vehicles)* were fitted to some American ICBMs in the early 1960s. They replaced one large warhead with several smaller ones which when they reach their target scatter like bits of shrapnel and hit several different targets.

During the 1960s one threat to the ability of ICBMs to reach their targets was the proposed anti-ballistic missile (ABM). It was thought that ABMs could destroy incoming missiles before they could do any damage. ABM systems were never developed to any great extent, but the answer to them was the *MIRV (Multiple Independently Targetable Re-entry Vehicle).*

So powerful is the weaponry aboard nuclear submarines that, for example, the British Government believes that the mere threat of the use of the missiles from just one of the Navy's Polaris submarines would be enough to prevent the Russians or anyone else from attacking this country.

Until anti-submarine warfare techniques catch up with the nuclear submarine it remains the most powerful reason why no one can hope to win a war through a surprise first attack.

The newest development in SLBMs is the

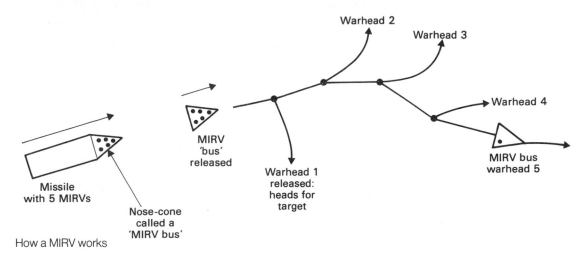

How a MIRV works

A MIRV like a MRV carries several warheads, but they are not released in a random or scattered way. They are released separately and can be aimed at different targets, sometimes hundreds of miles apart. Most ICBMs and SLBMs are today 'MIRVed'.

MIRVs meant that the United States and the Soviet Union were able to increase their nuclear arsenals greatly whilst limiting their numbers of missiles.

MARV (Manoeuvrable Alternatively Targetable Re-entry Vehicle) is similar to MIRV except that each MARVed missile warhead can, after firing, alter its course to avoid any defensive action taken against it. Trident D5 will probably be MARVed.

The Cruise Missile

The latest addition to the missile armoury, *Cruise,* is not a ballistic missile but a self-guiding one, directed to its target by an on-board computer. It is like a small, pilotless aircraft; flying low to avoid radar it is accurate to within 90 feet. It has a range of up to 2000 miles and carries a warhead fifteen times more powerful than the Hiroshima bomb.

Cruise can be launched from almost any platform: aircraft, surface ships, submarines and transporter vehicles on roads. Cruise, unlike other delivery systems is relatively cheap to produce and therefore it will probably become very plentiful.

The most important thing about Cruise is that although it is slow (it flies below the speed of sound), it is claimed to be undetectable by present-day radar systems. This means that it can strike targets without giving any warning and so it is possible to think about starting a nuclear war with a hope of winning it; something that other missiles do not give.

American cruise missiles have been sited in Britain at Greenham Common in Berkshire and during 1986 they will be in place at Molesworth in Cambridgeshire;

also, they are to be sited in other countries of Western Europe.

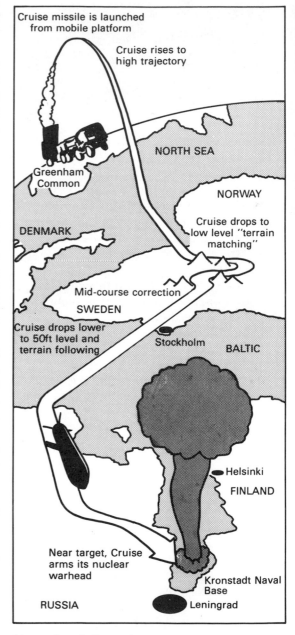

How cruise missiles work

The Nuclear Delivery Systems of the USA and the USSR

	Long-Range or Strategic Weapons			
	USA		**USSR**	
Bombers	316		145	
Total number of nuclear weapons carried by bombers		2570		290
ICBMs				
Missiles	1051		1398	
Warheads		2151		5678
SLBMs				
Missiles	544		937	
Warheads		4960		2813
Total number of long-range bombers and missiles	1911		2480	
Total number of warheads		9681		8781
Total megatons	3488		6656	

(Source: *SIPRI Yearbook*, 1983.)

Nuclear Warheads in Europe

		The Western Alliance (NATO)	The Warsaw Pact (USSR)
Long-Range (more than 1000 miles)			
Land-based	French	16	766
Submarine	Polaris: British ⎫ M20: French ⎬ Poseidon: USA ⎭	465	0
Aircraft		216	372
Long-Range total		697	1138
Medium-Range (100 to 1000 miles)			
Land-based		162	618
Submarine		0	26
Aircraft		340	515
Medium-Range total		502	1159
Short-Range (less than 100 miles)		6000	3500
Grand total all warheads		7199	5797

(Source: ISS 'The Military Balance' 1982–83. *SIPRI Yearbook*, 1983.)

Note: France is not a member of the military part of the Western Alliance and so has independent control of its weapons. However, the Russians regard themselves as the target for the French missiles and therefore they are included in the Western Alliance column.

Tactical and theatre nuclear weapons

In addition to ICBMs and SLBMs and Cruise there are many more nuclear missiles, mostly based in Europe, under American or Russian control. These weapons have shorter ranges than ICBMs; they are meant for use in a nuclear war in the European 'theatre'.

Think-time and missiles

The 'shrinking world' effect caused by the increasing efficiency of transport systems has brought great benefits to many people, but it has brought only one thing to military planners — dangerous problems.

'Think-time' is a phrase which means the amount of time you have to react to a certain situation; the amount of time you have to decide what to do.

A goalkeeper watches the opposing keeper kick the ball high into the air, over one hundred yards away. The goalkeeper has time to think as the ball comes down quite slowly. But when the ball drops at the feet of the opposing side's striker only a few yards away the keeper has to think and move very quickly.

From a time when delivery systems took hours to reach targets, in the 1950s, we now have the situation where think-time is down to fifteen minutes in the case of ICBMs launched from Russia or America. Weapons fired in Europe can reduce think-time to as low as six minutes.

The effects of the steady decrease in think-time are as follows:

a) Launch-on-warning threats. Both the United States and the Soviet Union have said that it is now possible that as soon as their radars show unidentified objects on their screens they might not bother checking to see what the objects are, as they have always done in the past. They claim that they will not have the time to sort out the difference between harmless objects and a hail of missiles. Rather than take the risk of losing their own missiles in a surprise attack they could launch their missiles on warning alone.

b) Computer systems already warn of an attack. It is said that because think-time is now so short, computers may eventually displace the people who order the missiles to be fired. Machines will not only warn of attack, but they will also be responsible for ordering the counter-attack.

TASK: Chapter 7

You are a trade union official and you are aware of the terrible effects of nuclear weapons. Your company has just received an important defence contract — work on nuclear submarines which the shipyard needs to avoid redundancies.

Would you accept the contract? Or would you reject it?

How would you justify your decision?

8   Control of nuclear weapons

C3

We mentioned earlier that the land-based ICBMs are considered vulnerable to surprise attack and that although submarines are usually safe from detection, advances in anti-submarine warfare could make them vulnerable. However, the *most vulnerable* and *most valuable* part of a nuclear weapons system is called *command, communication* and *control* or C3.

C3 is like a brain, it sends messages to all other parts of the body; it controls all movements; knock out the brain and the other parts of the body are helpless. C3 provides the essential information needed by the people at the top to control their forces during a war; it also can provide a line of communication with an enemy.

The massive network of C3 is made up of radar and radio stations throughout the world. The electromagnetic pulse (EMP) from a nuclear explosion high in the earth's atmosphere could destroy C3, leaving the people who are supposed to control events without any knowledge of what is happening.

Nuclear weapons are spread over many countries and places and are in the hands of the men in the missile silos, the sailors aboard the ships and submarines, the pilots in the bombers and local battlefield commanders.

What might happen if C3 was destroyed either during or at the start of a war?

The decision whether or not to use nuclear weapons would be left to the thousands of people who control them locally. They would receive no orders from the top; they would have to act on their own initiative. How would they know if the breakdown of C3 was accidental or part of a real attack?

No one person on a battlefield, in a plane or on a submarine can fire a nuclear weapon; others are needed to help. What would these groups decide to do after a breakdown of C3 — nothing? Or would they assume the worst and fire their weapons?

This has never happened — yet.

Note: The Return of the Doomsday Machine
The increasing vulnerability of nuclear weapons has brought about a return of the idea of the Doomsday Machine. The latest

C3 malfunction

version says that nuclear weapons could be taken and hidden, safely, deep in outer space. Their return to earth would be triggered either by a command from earth or by a failure to give that command. No enemy would dare attack knowing that within a few hours or days after the attack a massive rain of nuclear destruction would come down on them from out of the deep reaches of space.

The People Who Fire the Weapons

The control and use of nuclear weapons, as we have seen, can be in the hands of many people. The need for stable, well-balanced human beings who can make quick, controlled decisions is essential.

Submarine, bomber and missile crews undergo lengthy and complicated tests to try to make sure that they (a) fire their weapons when they are told to, and (b) do not fire them until they are told to.

The problem with using people instead of machines to control nuclear weapons is that they have feelings. From the military point of view nothing ought to divert a missile crew from firing when ordered to. They must never be allowed to consider exactly what they are doing, that is, slaughtering innocent people hundreds or thousands of miles away.

Ordinary people, who apparently have no serious mental abnormalities can be made to kill others provided someone in authority tells them to and the killing is at a distance. Pressing a button to fire a missile, on the orders of a superior, to bring death to other people is far easier to do than asking someone to go out and knife an innocent human being. The first is called *duty,* the second is *murder*: but they are both *killings.*

We do not know a great deal about the other side of the story; people who have tried to fire missiles or drop bombs without orders.

TASK: Chapter 8

You are the captain of a missile-firing submarine. C3 suddenly breaks down; you have lost contact with your superiors; the electromagnetic pulse (EMP) caused by a nuclear explosion has created this situation; you know this, but what you don't know is whether the explosion was accidental or part of a nuclear attack on your country.

Immediately after the explosion you detect an enemy submarine heading in your direction; it will soon be near enough to attack you if it wants to. There is no chance of resuming contact with your superiors.

Remember that you are under orders to fire your missiles at the enemy's cities in the case of nuclear war.

What course of action would you take? And why?

9   Targets

Who and What Will Be on the Receiving End of the Bombs

Twenty-five years ago the targets for nuclear weapons were the cities and towns of Europe, America and Russia which would be laid waste and the people in them destroyed.

Today, the United States has 40 000 Soviet targets that it believes ought to be hit and destroyed in a nuclear war. The target list is neatly divided into four sections:

a)   Soviet nuclear forces, 2000 targets;
b)   other military targets, 20 000;
c)   Soviet military and political leadership centres, 3000 targets; and
d)   economic and industrial targets, 15 000.

The Russians will have a similar list for American and European targets.

Advances in missile technology have made it possible to hit, with a high degree of accuracy, nearly every target you want to hit.

Not a single city or town is listed for destruction. This seems a hopeful sign until you realise that because buildings, like factories, are seldom situated miles from towns but close to or within them there is little hope of survival for the peoples of America, Russia and Europe. The American target list means that 80 per cent of Russian towns and cities would be hit. The deaths of the people in them is counted as 'collateral damage'.

Doubtless the Russians could inflict similar collateral damage on the Americans and Europeans.

What the list really means is that nearly everything and everybody is a nuclear target.

10　Warning of nuclear attack

From Fylingdales Moor in north Yorkshire across the Atlantic Ocean to Greenland and through Canada to the frozen wastes of Alaska stretches the Ballistic Missile Early Warning System (BMEWS). An invisible, but complete radar line; cross it and you will be picked up by the computers of the United States North American Air Defence (NORAD) in Colorado.

And above BMEWS, satellite sensors in space probe the great landmass of the Soviet Union for all signs of military activity. BMEWS gives the United States fifteen minutes to decide what to do about anything crossing that line; it gives Britain about four minutes to decide its actions.

NORAD has a direct link to the President of the United States; the only person who can officially order missiles and bombers to attack Soviet targets. The 'hotline', a telex link between America and Russia, provides

Fylingdales ballistic missile early warning station

a direct communication between the President and the leadership of the Soviet Union. It is meant for use to avoid nuclear war by accident.

BMEWS, other warning systems and the hotline seem to ensure that accidental war cannot happen; and yet in November 1979, and again in June 1980, the BMEWS system failed and signalled a massive nuclear attack on the United States. US forces around the world went on alert. The error was discovered in time, before a single ICBM silo could open or before a single SLBM could be primed for lift-off.

Up to October 1980, BMEWS recorded 147 false alarms.

BMEWS covers the approaches to North America over the top of the world. It is from this direction across the North Pole that a Russian missile and bomber attack would come; it is the shortest route between the United States and the Soviet Union.

When an alert happens, aeroplanes have an important part to play. Fighter planes can check out any unauthorised intruders and the bombers can take off and fly towards Soviet airspace. This is one of the reasons bombers have been kept because by their actions they show the other side that you are aware that something has crossed the radar line and additionally they can be recalled to base once the alert is over.

Missiles serve no purpose in the early warning system; they cannot be launched to show the other side that you are aware of intruders, because once they are fired they cannot be called back.

The failures by the computers of the early

warning system can show two things:

a) just how good a 'back-up' system the Americans have because they discovered the alarms to be false ones — in time; and

b) how reliance on a machine could lead to nuclear war by accident.

The Soviet Union has its own system to match the Americans; peering across the ice-packs of the North Pole.

favourite programme is starting; the oven which refuses to work on Christmas morning; the washing machine which floods in the night; these and numerous other domestic calamities are examples of 'Murphy's Law'.

These failures might cause you and your family annoyance, frustration or distress. However, they do not usually affect the lives of others.

Breakdowns in some systems do affect

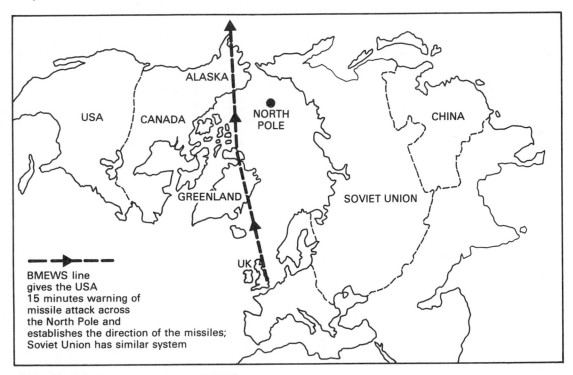

— — — —▶
BMEWS line
gives the USA
15 minutes warning of
missile attack across
the North Pole and
establishes the direction of the missiles;
Soviet Union has similar system

Ballistic missile early warning system – BMEWS

TASK: Chapter 10

Modern society's reliance on complicated machinery brings a fresh meaning to the everyday notion known as 'Murphy's Law', which says that 'if anything can go wrong, it will'. Perhaps we should add a further phrase, 'and when you least want it to'. Things like the television failing just as your

the lives of thousands or even millions of people.

In 1979, at Three Mile Island nuclear power station in the United States, a nuclear reactor failed. The lives of many people were put at risk. Nuclear safety experts had claimed (before the incident) that you were more likely to be hit by a meteor than suffer the effects of a nuclear reactor breakdown!

Complete system breakdowns can be caused by failures in small parts of the system. The alarm (mentioned in the previous chapter) which falsely signalled a massive nuclear attack on the United States was caused by *one* microchip failure in the American early warning system — the chip cost 25p.

A single failure in a country's nuclear early warning system is unlikely to start a war. However, when several things go wrong at the same time the danger of an accidental slide into nuclear war would be heightened, particularly if great tension existed between enemies.

Suppose your enemy's early warning system fails for a short period and during this failure one of your own missiles is launched accidentally; it reaches its target and destroys a major city.

Form two groups, A and B.

Group A has to convince Group B that the missile launch was an accident. They can start by saying that if the launch was deliberate they could have used the breakdown of the early warning system to destroy the enemy *completely*.

Group B could start by replying that the loss of a major city and its population *may* have been an accident, but (a) accidents can happen again and (b) their people are outraged and demand some sort of action.

What can Group A do to convince Group B that the launch was accidental? And what will Group B do if Group A's explanation does not satisfy them?

11   Defence against nuclear weapons

There is no real defence against nuclear weapons; most missiles launched will reach their targets. There are, however, two ways you can try to reduce the full effects of a nuclear attack.

One way is to try to stop some nuclear weapons reaching their targets; this is called **active defence**. The other method is to do as much as possible to protect your country from the effects of the weapons after they have hit their targets; this is called **passive** or **civil defence**.

Civil Defence

Civil defence concentrates on two ways to protect people; one is by building shelters, the other by evacuating people away from target areas.

There are two main types of shelter: (a) heat- and blast-proof shelters, and (b) radioactive fallout shelters.

Heat and blast shelters are not usually available to ordinary people; they are very costly and therefore only within the reach of the rich, leading politicians and the military. However, fallout shelters are not so costly to construct. In Britain, the Government has issued a pamphlet called *Protect and Survive* which gives details of how to build a fallout shelter in your own home.

Evacuation of people from target areas would involve a huge planning operation. There would have to be food, water and housing provided for them in the places they were sent to; and fallout shelters would also need to be built.

Building a fallout shelter in your own home

Civil defence in Britain is dealt with in later chapters, but we can say some general things about it now.

Evacuation plans depend on being warned about a nuclear war; they are useless without time to carry out the plans. Most countries in the world do not bother to even consider evacuation as a way of protection. Evacuation also depends for its effectiveness on having 'safe areas' to send people to. A safe area is one that has no or acceptable levels of radioactive fallout. In a small country, like Britain, safe areas would be very difficult to find.

Most available shelters give some protection against radioactive fallout; again like evacuation they depend on warning time. Unless you have already built one, how long would it take to make one? Would you do it properly? And would it really save your life considering you would have to stay in it for at least fourteen days with food, drink and lavatory facilities available?

The British Government believes that millions of people would survive a nuclear attack and go on surviving if only they would follow the instructions given in *Protect and Survive.*

As we have seen, surviving a nuclear war would be very difficult for people in target areas; but even if you did survive what kind of life would you have afterwards? All the predictions seem to be that no matter how you protect yourself against the actual attack you will then be faced with trying to survive in impossible circumstances. Shelters may therefore only be a method of keeping you alive a little longer than those killed in a nuclear attack.

Active Defence

Active defence against nuclear weapons means, as we have seen, preventing nuclear warheads reaching their targets; that involves knocking out as many bombers and missiles as you can while they are in flight.

Most of the destructive power of nuclear weapons is carried on missiles; and as these are the most difficult to stop reaching their targets active defence ideas and systems are concerned mainly with them.

How do you stop a nuclear missile in flight? During the 1960s there was much talk about anti-missiles; missiles launched with the intention of destroying incoming missiles in the earth's upper atmosphere by exploding close to them and so knocking them out. These anti-missiles came to be called anti-ballistic missiles or ABMs.

There are, however, many problems associated with ABMs:

a) the cost of building ABMs to match the number of expected enemy missiles is astronomical;
b) the enemy might fire false or decoy missiles to confuse your ABMs;
c) the enemy might put many warheads on one missile to swamp your ABMs; and
d) the enemy could 'underfly' your ABM system using low-flying cruise-missiles.

But the most important problem is to do with *certainty of destruction*. In 1967, the American President, Lyndon Johnson, called together his scientific advisers and asked them whether an ABM system would

work. Johnson wanted to know if such a system would work *all of the time* and if they could be *certain* it would destroy all incoming missiles; because even if a few got through the destruction would be enormous.

The answer he got was: No!

The problems with ABMs led the United States and the Soviet Union to sign the Anti-Ballistic Missile Treaty in 1972. This banned the setting up of more than two such systems on each side. A few years later they agreed to reduce the number to one each side, consisting of only one hundred launchers. These could be placed around their capital cities or used to protect missile launching sites. The Americans did not build their system, but the Russians did install one around Moscow; this is now out-of-date.

The issue of active defence seemed to be dead and buried; now suddenly in the 1980s it has been revived. The American President, Ronald Reagan, gave what has been called his 'Star Wars' speech, in which he announced that the United States was planning new defence measures for use in the future. These new measures are not only based on the previous idea of anti-ballistic missiles, but on technical advances based mainly on laser beams mounted on satellites high above the earth. The official name used to describe Star Wars is the 'Strategic Defense Initiative'.

The American space shuttle would be used to transport satellites into space where they would lie in wait for enemy missiles. A laser beam, moving at the speed of light, would strike the missiles and burn them up.

In 1980 the United States Air Force announced it had successfully tested a laser weapon capable of destroying missiles; it even exhibited the remains of a target destroyed by a laser at the Farnborough Air Show in 1980.

The reasons put forward by the Americans for wanting to produce these 'killer-satellites' are:

a) the Russians are developing them;
b) nuclear missiles will reach their targets and so any system which promises to prevent this is a good idea; and
c) if *both* sides do develop effective killer-satellites this will mean that there will be no point in having nuclear weapons and this could lead to nuclear disarmament.

Even if killer-satellites were possible technically (and there are many obstacles to overcome), the enemy, provided they themselves do not possess these satellites, will be forced to make certain choices to deal with them.

Suppose either the Americans or Russians were on the point of having an effective system, what could the other side do about this believing that their own missiles would soon no longer reach their targets? They could:

a) start a nuclear war and hope to win it before their missiles became useless;
b) toughen the 'skins' of their missiles to stop laser beams penetrating and so force the other side to spend more money to develop a stronger laser; or
c) launch their own satellites to hunt

down and destroy the other side's killer-satellites.

Killer-satellites, with lethal lasers, are a suggestion for the future, but the idea of them has caused problems for Western European countries. It is feared that the intention of this active defence system is to destroy missiles fired at the United States not those fired at Britain and the rest of Europe. We would remain unprotected. This would be seen as a sign that the Americans did not take seriously their promise to defend Europe in case of attack by the Russians.

Whether an active defence system is based on ABMs or lasers or any other technical wonder, there still remains the problem of certainty. Would any President of the United States or leader of the Soviet Union ever be *certain* that the defence system would be effective under attack conditions? Because if it was not effective the consequence is mutual and massive nuclear destruction.

Note: The Outer Space Treaty of 1967 expressly forbids the destruction of satellites by any sort of weapon. The Anti-Ballistic Missile Treaty of 1972 prohibits setting up lasers or particle beams in an anti-ballistic missile role. However, this treaty does not ban their development.

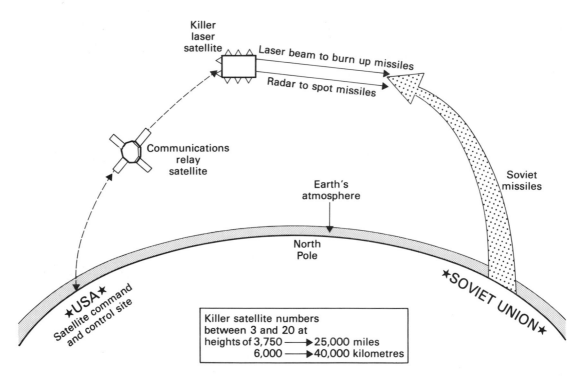

How the killer satellites would work – American version

12 The proliferation of nuclear weapons

Proliferation means to increase rapidly: to spread. The proliferation of nuclear weapons happens in two forms; one with an increase in the number of weapons by the countries who already have nuclear weapons. For example, the increased number of warheads resulting from the MIRVing of ICBMs is proliferation.

The other form of proliferation means the spread of nuclear weapons to countries other than those who already possess them; and it is this we will now consider.

Proliferation started as soon as the United States ceased to be the only country to have nuclear weapons when the Soviet Union got the bomb in 1949. Countries known to have nuclear weapons in addition to America and Russia are Britain, France, China and India.

Has anyone else got the bomb? Who else could make the bomb? Pakistan, Israel and South Africa are strongly suspected of having nuclear weapons; just how many, what sort they are and the kinds of delivery systems they have are not generally known.

In addition to this group there are two other categories:

a)   those who are suspected of constructing atomic weapons; and
b)   those who have the facilities to make weapons, but are not thought to be making them.

'HOW COME THEY CAN PLAY WITH THEM, BUT WE CAN'T?'

The list below shows the situation as it is known.

PROLIFERATION OF NUCLEAR WEAPONS

COUNTRIES THAT HAVE NUCLEAR WEAPONS
USA, USSR, BRITAIN, FRANCE, CHINA and INDIA

COUNTRIES SUSPECTED OF ALREADY HAVING NUCLEAR WEAPONS
PAKISTAN, ISRAEL and SOUTH AFRICA.

COUNTRIES SUSPECTED OF MAKING NUCLEAR WEAPONS
ARGENTINA, BRAZIL, EGYPT, IRAQ, LIBYA, SOUTH KOREA AND TAIWAN.

COUNTRIES THAT COULD MAKE NUCLEAR WEAPONS IF THEY WANTED TO
AUSTRIA, AUSTRALIA, BELGIUM, BULGARIA, CANADA, CHILE, COLUMBIA, CUBA, CZECHOSLOVAKIA, DENMARK, FINLAND, WEST GERMANY, EAST GERMANY, GREECE, HUNGARY, INDONESIA, IRAN, ITALY, JAPAN, MEXICO, NETHERLANDS, NORTH KOREA, NORWAY, PHILIPPINES, POLAND, PORTUGAL, RUMANIA, SPAIN, SWEDEN, SWITZERLAND, THAILAND, TURKEY, URUGUAY, VENEZUELA, YUGOSLAVIA, ZAIRE.

(Sources: International Atomic Energy Agency *Annual Report* 1981, Vienna; *SIPRI Yearbook,* 1981.)

How Countries Get the Bomb

As we have seen, nuclear weapons can be made from two substances, Uranium$_{235}$ and Plutonium$_{239}$. The usual way to get nuclear weapons is by building nuclear reactors for use in power stations. Pu$_{239}$ is a by-product of the process in nuclear reactors and U$_{235}$ is used as the fuel in a reactor. So by getting nuclear power stations a country can gain the products needed for nuclear weapons. The process of production (the nuclear fuel cycle) which results in U$_{235}$ and Pu$_{239}$ is relatively cheap and widely known.

Until 1985, the manufacture of U$_{235}$ for use in nuclear weapons needed several thousand distinct stages. However the United States has announced that it now has the capability to produce U$_{235}$ in a *single* operation housed in a building no larger than an ordinary barn.

The other material used in nuclear weapons manufacture — Pu$_{239}$ — is in greater demand by the military because it is more compact and has more power for its size than does U$_{235}$. Pu$_{239}$ could be made by the same new process as U$_{235}$.

The new technology is based on the use of lasers in U$_{235}$ and Pu$_{239}$ manufacture. It is called Atomic Vapour Laser Isotope Separation (AVLIS).

Although the US has a ten-year lead in this technology, its cheapness and ease of production can only mean that any country in the world could afford nuclear weapons.

Such is the concern felt by many nations about the spread of nuclear weapons that a Non-Proliferation Treaty was agreed in 1968; eventually 115 nations signed it. (Part of this treaty is given at the end of this section.)

There are four major problems associated with the Non-Proliferation Treaty (NPT).

1. Some countries who have the bomb or are suspected of having it or thought to be making it have not signed the treaty. France, China and India have refused to sign. Pakistan, Israel and South Africa who are already thought to have the bomb have not signed. Argentina and Brazil who are thought to be constructing the bomb have not signed either.
2. The treaty says that all countries who

do not have the bomb should allow inspectors working for the International Atomic Energy Agency (IAEA) to visit them to keep track of all nuclear materials that could be used to make a bomb. However, the IAEA cannot *force* countries to do as it wants; it has no real power.

3. The NPT allows countries who have signed it to withdraw from it whenever they want; it is not a permanent agreement.
4. What is most surprising of all about a treaty that is supposed to prevent the spread of nuclear weapons is that it allows the development of nuclear technology for peaceful purposes and yet this is the usual way countries acquire nuclear weapons.

The best thing that can be said about the NPT is that it at least shows that countries realise the dangers involved in the spread of nuclear weapons and that it is evidence of their will to act to try to do something about it.

The worst thing that can be said about it is that it seems like a weak attempt by the major nuclear countries to keep nuclear weapons in a 'closed shop' controlled by them.

Why Other Countries Want the Bomb

1. Nuclear weapons are the cheapest and most effective method of mass slaughter ever invented. They cannot for very long be kept out of the hands of any country that wants them; they are too tempting.
2. 'They've got them; why shouldn't we have them.' It is very difficult for the countries who already have nuclear weapons to think of a good reason to persuade others not to get them. It is all very well saying that nuclear weapons are dangerous and their spread is a bad thing. A country that does not have the bomb can always reply: 'If they are that bad why don't you get rid of yours?'
3. A country may feel threatened by another country and so gets the bomb to put off any threat against itself.
4. A country may believe that an enemy is in the process of constructing nuclear weapons and so feels it necessary to build their own as a deterrent.
5. Countries might think that if they have nuclear weapons they will become more important in their region or throughout the world. They might feel that with the bomb they will have to be taken seriously.

It is important and also worrying to note that those countries already suspected of having nuclear weapons (Pakistan, Israel and South Africa) are ones who are involved in long-standing disputes with their neighbours; quarrels which have, at times, spilled over into acts of terrorism or all-out war.

Israel is surrounded by Arab countries which are, in the main, hostile to it. South Africa, which is controlled by a white minority, is enclosed by countries which want to see an end to white domination in Southern Africa. Pakistan has been in dispute with neighbouring India over the control of Kashmir.

The temptation to settle old or new arguments between countries using nuclear weapons might be just too much for some of them.

Perhaps it is too late to put a brake on the spread of nuclear weapons. At first the United States and the Soviet Union, acting together, might have done this, but for many countries the race to have the bomb is well underway.

Dangers of the Spread of Nuclear Weapons

What might happen when so many countries have nuclear weapons? Here are some worries.

1. Before the existence of nuclear weapons when countries had sudden and unexpected quarrels it took some time for those quarrels to spill over into open war. It took time to get ready to fight; armies had to be assembled in battle order; by then the hot tempers brought on by the sudden and unexpected quarrels may have cooled and a decision not to go to war may have been made.

   Nuclear weapons have changed this situation, for they allow almost *instant* attack on an enemy. The mere push of a button or the turning of a key or a short flight by jet aircraft can bring down destruction on an enemy. They do away with cooling-off periods.

2. If you know an enemy has nuclear weapons or is on the point of getting them you might be tempted to attack before that enemy can attack you.

3. The possession of nuclear weapons could lead countries to neglect non-nuclear or conventional armaments because they are cheaper and give a 'bigger bang for a buck'. A situation might then come about where a relatively trivial or minor outbreak of violence would have to be settled either by surrender or nuclear war. There would be no half-way house solution because a country, through neglect, had not got sufficient non-nuclear forces to deal with the problem.

4. Countries that depend on machines to warn them of an attack must expect those machines to occasionally fail or give misleading information. We have seen that the United States with all its experience of high technology has had computer failures which gave wrong information about nuclear attacks.

   What happens when many countries not only have weapons and delivery systems but computerised early warning systems? Can they be expected to operate at the same 'high standards' as the American equipment?

   The spread of nuclear weapons will increase the danger of accidental nuclear war many times over through the possibility of the failure of early warning systems. Uncertainty about what is really happening could prompt a country to fire its missiles 'just in case'.

5. We have said before that nuclear weapons are relatively cheap; many large companies or even some individuals could afford them if any country was immoral enough to sell them; cruise missiles now provide not just cheap warheads but an inexpensive delivery system.

6. Once nuclear weapons are more widely spread it makes the working-out of arms control agreements very difficult; also it would become almost impossible to check up to see if anyone was breaking an agreement.

7. In history, large and powerful countries, before they have attacked smaller ones, have nearly always needed an excuse to do so; a reason to justify their attack so that the rest of the world sees them as the 'goodies' and the countries under attack as the 'baddies'. Even someone as ruthless as Adolf Hitler always invented some 'good' reason for his attacks.

   Nuclear weapons in the possession of small countries would make it easier for big countries to attack them. They provide the perfect cover-story for what might have been a long-standing intention to attack them anyway.

8. *Who Fired that Missile at us?*

   If a country's early warning system picks up nuclear missiles heading for it that country must assume that its main enemy has launched an attack on it. The United States, for example, would assume that the Russians had attacked. But did they? Might not another country with a grudge against both America and Russia arrange for it to look like that? This is called catalytic war; when a third country acts to cause a war between two other countries.

The world already faces destruction because of the rivalry of the major nuclear powers, the United States and the Soviet Union. How much more devastation and how much closer will that devastation be when nuclear weapons spread to many other nations?

The Non-Proliferation Treaty (Main Articles) 1968

Article 1 forbids the transfer of nuclear weapons or explosives either directly or indirectly from the nuclear weapons States to anyone else.

Article 2 bans non-nuclear weapons States from getting or developing nuclear weapons.

Article 3 says that non-nuclear weapons States have to accept safeguards operated by the International Atomic Energy Agency over their civilian nuclear programmes to make sure that no nuclear weapons material is diverted for military use.

Article 4 says that all States have the right to develop nuclear power for peaceful purposes.

Article 10 says that countries have the right to withdraw from the treaty after giving three months' notice.

THE DANGERS OF NUCLEAR PROLIFERATION

1. NO TIME FOR TEMPERS TO COOL: THE BOMB CAN MEAN INSTANT RESPONSE

2. AN ENEMY GETS THE BOMB

3. ALL CONFLICTS SETTLED BY USING THE BOMB.

4. MORE EARLY WARNING SYSTEMS MEAN MORE CHANCE OF ACCIDENTAL WAR

5. THEY ARE CHEAP SO THEY CAN SPREAD TO COMPANIES OR INDIVIDUALS.

6. ARMS CONTROL AND DISARMAMENT BECOME MORE DIFFICULT.

7. THE BIG PEOPLE FIND AN EXCUSE TO ATTACK THE LITTLE PEOPLE

8. CATALYTIC WAR BY THIRD PARTY

13 Arms control and disarmament

We are here to make a choice between the quick and the dead. We must elect world peace or world destruction.
(Bernard Baruch, 14 August 1946.)

Do not confuse arms control with disarmament; they can be very different things. Arms control means that countries agree to *control* their armaments; they may agree to a *controlled increase* or *decrease* in armaments.

Disarmament means a gradual reduction, by phases, of all weapons of war until no such weapons exist. Disarmament can only be successfully achieved when at the end of the process all the nations involved feel *secure* from attack.

When arms control or disarmament is discussed reductions in nuclear weaponry usually top the list as they are the most deadly weapons in the world.

Arms control and disarmament talks when reported by the press or television are a bewildering series of claims and counterclaims often dragging on for years and very often ending in total breakdown. Too many talks have followed this pattern since 1945; sometimes the United States is the guilty party; sometimes the Soviet Union.

Why do Countries Talk about Arms Control and Disarmament?

1. Pressure of public opinion; the peoples of the world do not want to see their lives ended by a nuclear holocaust. Politicians, therefore, have to be seen to be doing something about nuclear armaments. Even in Russia, where public opinion is not freely expressed, the leadership knows that the Russian people do not want another war.

2. Politicians may genuinely want to see arms control and disarmament achieved and go ahead on this basis.

3. Leaders may realise that they have all the weapons they need; to go on producing more would be wasteful. They might, therefore, negotiate arms control on a particular weapon so that they can divert the money that would have been used on it to some other purpose. Unfortunately, diverting funds can mean creating some new kind of weapon.

4. The arms race is costly; so expensive that no one can really put a figure on future development costs. A country realising this might want to come to an agreement simply to put a brake on expenditure costs.

False discussions

Arms control and disarmament talks are either genuine or false. A false negotiation happens when a country is forced to do something to look good in the eyes of its own people, or its friends, or the rest of the world. It may start talks to achieve a propaganda victory. It does this by producing offers which it knows the other side will refuse; and when the other side rejects these offers it throws its hands in the air and says, 'Just look how unreasonable the other side is; rejecting our offers; how can you negotiate with people like that?' Having achieved its propaganda victory the country that made the offers goes on to produce more weapons, claiming they have been forced to by lack of co-operation from the other side.

The leaders of countries involved in arms control and disarmament talks do not participate in them on a day-to-day basis. Leaders tend to meet only at the beginning of talks when they try to agree to an agenda for the talks, or at the end when they formally sign any agreement that has been reached. The meeting, in November 1985, between Ronald Reagan, the President of the United States, and Mikhail Gorbachev, the leader of the Soviet Union, came at a time when full-scale arms control and disarmament talks had just resumed between their two countries. One of the main purposes of the Reagan–Gorbachev summit meeting was to establish the major areas for negotiation between the United States and the Soviet Union.

Genuine discussions

Will — Confidence Building — Trust — Verification

These are the four keys to genuine, successful and lasting disarmament.

Suppose that for many years you have lived in fear of your enemy; the distrust between you has been so intense that, at times, you have been on the point of open conflict. Now you are both genuinely fed up with living with the day-to-day worry of open war. You decide to do something about it; you agree to talk about disarmament. Both of you have the *will* to seek an agreement.

The first thing you need to know is what kind and how many armaments the other side has. Figures have been produced about weapons which may have been totally untrue or inflated just to impress you.

The other side gives you a big list and says that the amounts and kinds of weaponry on it are true. Can you *trust* the other side? You have been enemies for a long time; it would be silly to rely on the figures on a list and nothing else. You need to feel *confident* that you are being told the truth and the only way to do that is to be able to *verify* what has been given you. Verification means to check the truth of something.

If you have the will to negotiate a genuine agreement and are able to satisfy yourself about the truth of the other side's list then your confidence in their word will increase and trust will start to build between you.

You are now able to begin to disarm and provided you can continue to verify information given to you then confidence and trust will increase and a phased and gradual disarmament can be the result.

The only other problem you will face is what to do about the other people who possess weapons who have not been involved in your discussions. You cannot disarm and leave other people armed and able to attack you. Disarmament depends on a country feeling safe once it has disarmed. It needs its *security* safeguarded.

You and the other side must make sure that other countries disarm; you can do this in a number of ways:

a) *by example;* other nations might possess weapons because they are frightened of you; the fact that you are disarming could persuade them to do the same thing and provided they can verify your actions they will feel confident that they will be secure when disarmed.

b) *forced disarmament;* it may be that some countries refuse to disarm along with you. They may believe that if they keep their armaments then they can blackmail you and others. It is clear that any agreement on total, as opposed to nuclear, disarmament must involve nearly all countries of the world if it is to have any real meaning.

Disarmament, when achieved, is not the end of the story; *a permanent verification* system must be set up. For what will happen in the future when promises you made are forgotten or ignored by others? Knowledge of nuclear weapons and how to build them will always be with us; a permanent verification system would have to ensure that such knowledge is never again used to construct weapons of mass destruction. Disarmament would not stop with nuclear weapons, others such as chemical and biological weapons would have to be dealt with. After these come conventional weapons. However, it might be wishful thinking to pretend that all conventional weapons would ever disappear.

We have seen how genuine disarmament would proceed, but unfortunately the conditions necessary to achieve it have hardly begun. Talk of confidence, trust and verification has always foundered on the mutual distrust of the United States and the Soviet Union; and it is only these countries that can make disarmament work. They have most of the world's nuclear weapons and until they start genuine disarmament negotiations the world will go on living in fear of destruction.

Steps to End the Nuclear Arms Race

Politicians and other leaders have suggested some definite steps to put an end to the nuclear arms race. The most important of these is the suggestion for a 'nuclear freeze' which says:

> To improve national and international security the United States and the Soviet Union should stop the nuclear arms race. Specifically they should adopt a mutual freeze on testing, production and deployment of nuclear weapons and missiles and new aircraft designed primarily to deliver nuclear weapons. This is an essential verifiable first step towards lessening the risk of nuclear war and reducing arsenals.
> (From US 'Freeze' proposal *The Call to Halt the Nuclear Arms Race.*)

Other suggestions that would help to stop the nuclear arms race are given below:

- a complete nuclear test ban
- nuclear-free zones
- an agreement not to use nuclear weapons first in any war
- close down of production of nuclear weapons material, mainly U_{235} and Pu_{239}

At the end of this section you will see a list showing what has been achieved in arms control and disarmament since 1959; considering that the threat of mutual destruction hangs over each one of us it makes dismal reading.

Another suggestion to deal with the lack of progress in most arms control and disarmament talks has emerged in the form of unilateral nuclear disarmament; it is not a new idea. It has received most publicity in Britain and elsewhere in Western Europe.

Unilateral Nuclear Disarmament

This means *one-sided* disarmament; one side gives up its nuclear weapons in the hope that others will follow its example. Unilateral disarmament does not usually mean that a country is left helpless against attack, for in place of its nuclear armaments a country would invest its money in defence by ordinary or conventional weapons, with a fully-equipped armed force together with ordinary people trained to fight a guerrilla war against an invader or offer non-violent or passive resistance.

The suggestion for unilateral disarmament has come about from a feeling that the Americans and Russians have no serious intention to disarm, and that the nuclear arms race will, like all arms races before it, end in war; nuclear war. It is a suggestion which mixes hope with desperation. Somebody, somewhere, sometime has got to end the arms race and start to disarm. If the United States and the Soviet Union will not do anything then perhaps the example of another country, for instance Britain, giving up its nuclear arms will start the ball rolling.

The main objections to unilateral nuclear disarmament are:

a) other countries may not see it as an example to be followed, but as a sign of weakness; and

b) unilateral nuclear disarmament *sounds* bad. People might say: 'Why should we disarm when the others won't? Why should we start things off and leave ourselves open to attack? Let the Americans and Russians start things going.'

The issues raised by unilateral nuclear disarmament are dealt with more fully in Chapter 17.

> I am deeply saddened when I reflect on how little has been achieved in spite of all the talk there has been particularly about nuclear disarmament. There have been numerous international conferences and negotiations on the subject and we have all nursed dreams of a world at peace; but to no avail. Since the end of the Second World War, 34 years ago, we have had war after war. There is still armed conflict going on in several parts of the world. We live in an age of extreme peril because every war carries the danger that it could spread and involve the superpowers.

(Lord Louis Mountbatten, 11 May 1979, Strasbourg.)

Arms Control and Disarmament Agreements: Nuclear Weapons

To prevent the spread of nuclear weapons

Antarctic Treaty, 1959 bans military uses of the Antarctic; bans nuclear tests and nuclear waste dumping. (25)*

Outer Space Treaty, 1967 bans nuclear weapons in earth orbit and stationing in outer space. (81)

Latin American Nuclear Free Zone Treaty, 1967 bans testing, possession, deployment of nuclear weapons. All Latin American countries except Argentina, Brazil, Chile and Cuba have signed the treaty. (22)

Non-Proliferation Treaty, 1968 bans transfer of weapons or weapons technology to non-nuclear States. (118)

Seabed Treaty, 1971 bans nuclear weapons on the seabed beyond a 12-mile coastal limit. (70)

To reduce the risk of nuclear war

Hot Line and Modernisation Agreements, 1963 establishes direct radio and wire-telegraph links between Washington and Moscow to make sure that heads of government can communicate with each other in times of crisis. A second agreement in 1971 provided for satellite communication circuits. (USA and USSR)

Accident Measures Agreement, 1971 pledges the USA and the USSR to improve safeguards against accidental or unauthorised use of nuclear weapons. (USA and USSR)

Prevention of Nuclear War Agreement, 1973 requires consultation between USA and USSR if there is a danger of nuclear war.

*Number of countries that have signed the treaties.

48

To limit nuclear weapons testing

Partial Test Ban Treaty, 1963 bans nuclear weapons tests in the atmosphere, outer space, or underwater. Bans underground explosions which cause release of radioactive fallout beyond the country's borders. (111)

Threshold Test Ban Treaty, 1974 bans underground tests having a yield above 150 kilotons (150 000 tons of TNT equivalent). (USA and USSR)

Peaceful Nuclear Explosions Treaty, 1974 bans explosions with a combined yield of over 1500 kilotons. (USA and USSR)

To limit nuclear weapons

ABM (Anti-Ballistic Missile) Treaty, 1972 limits the number of ABM systems to two deployment areas on each side; later this was changed to one each side. (USA and USSR)

SALT I (Strategic Arms Limitation Treaty) 1972 freezes the number of strategic (long-range) ballistic missile launchers and permits an increase in SLBM (Submarine Launched Ballistic Missile) launchers up to an agreed level equivalent to the number of old ICBM or SLBM launchers dismantled. (USA and USSR)

SALT II, 1979** limits the number of strategic nuclear delivery vehicles; launchers of MIRVed missiles; bombers with long-range cruise missiles fitted; warheads on existing ICBMs. Bans testing or deployment of new ICBMs. (USA and USSR)

The Bomb — Right or Wrong

Would it be right to use nuclear weapons in a war? Is it wrong to even threaten to use them?

**SALT II agreed by the governments of America and Russia; but not agreed to by the American parliament (Congress) and so not a legally binding agreement.

Ever since violence was first used to settle disputes between countries, the issue of the rightness or wrongness of such actions has been the subject of debate. Most of the public comment has come from religious leaders. Over the years the Christian Church has developed the idea of the 'just war'; which says that *war itself* is not wrong, but *some* wars are right and *some* are wrong; some just, some unjust.

The Christian idea of the Just War contains two principles that have particular relevance to nuclear warfare. One is called the 'Principle of Proportion', which can be interpreted to mean that you must not inflict more damage than has been inflicted on you. For example, if an enemy has destroyed one small town it would be wrong to retaliate by destroying a large town.

The other is called the 'Principle of Discrimination', which says that it is wrong to kill innocent civilians or non-combatants in a war.

Such is the destructive power of nuclear weapons that these two principles really could not apply to a nuclear war. As we have seen there is no hope of nuclear weapons 'discriminating' between innocent civilians and soldiers and no real hope of their effects being kept in 'proportion'. The existence of nuclear weapons has led some people to believe that their use, because they break these two principles, is wrong or immoral.

It is in our view proven beyond reasonable doubt that the Just War theory, as this has developed in Western civilisation and within the Christian Church, rules out the use of nuclear weapons. The damage to non-combatants even indeed to neutral countries as unconnected with the quarrel as they are distant from the scene of operations; the havoc made of the environment; and the dangers to generations yet unborn; these things make nuclear weapons indiscriminate and nuclear war disproportionate. The evils caused by this method of making war are greater than any conceivable evil which the war is intended to prevent, and they affect

people who have nothing to do with the conflict.
(Source: *The Church and the Bomb: Nuclear Weapons and Christian Conscience,* working party under the Chairmanship of the Bishop of Salisbury, Hodder and Stoughton, 1982.)

If, according to one Christian view, the use of nuclear weapons is immoral then what about the *threat* to use them; is this right or wrong? There are two main views about this. One says that it is morally right to threaten to use them because this threat has kept the peace and prevented aggression over a number of years,

> War is evil; the prevention of war is a positive good. Possession of nuclear weapons ... deters others from threatening to use them. It would be immoral to leave one's country open to nuclear blackmail or attack.
> (Source: *The Nuclear Debate: Arms Control and Disarmament Research Unit,* Foreign and Commonwealth Office, London, 1982.)

The other view says that to threaten to use nuclear weapons is immoral because to do so means that a country must be prepared to use them should deterrence fail; therefore to threaten to use them is as morally wrong as their actual use.

> ... whatever we think of the use of nuclear weapons the threat to use them, in defence, is another matter. He offers a simple everyday analogy; the distinction we should all want to make between 'the man who threatens violence in defence of his own person or property and the man who does so in the commission of robbery or rape'. Perhaps we could take this analogy a little further. What should we say of a man who threatens that if physically assaulted he will burn his neighbour's wife and children to death?
> (Source: R. Gaskell, *Nuclear Weapons: The Way Ahead,* Menard Press, London, 1981.)

For a war to be just, according to the Christian Church, it has to be fought for certain reasons, for example, self-defence or freedom from oppression. Nuclear war may be wrong; to threaten a nuclear war is perhaps immoral, but do these things apply when a country is faced with an evil enemy? For example, is Communism so evil that nuclear war is justified to stop its spread or to crush it in the Soviet Union or China or elsewhere?

14   The arms race

An arms race is a continual effort to build up a stockpile of bigger and better weapons which you expect will keep you ahead of your enemies; that will make you superior to them and will make you safe from attack by them.

An ordinary race usually has a finish; a post or a tape which marks the end of the race. In an arms race the finishing post is never reached, it keeps moving further away from you. If an arms race does finish, history shows us that it will not end by reaching and passing a finishing post.

An arms race has three possible outcomes:

a)   it goes on and on for as far ahead as anyone can see;
b)   the people involved in the arms race negotiate an end to it; or
c)   the race ends in war; in the present day this means a nuclear war, a 'war to end all wars'.

The nuclear arms race costs a lot of money and it will go on costing more and more because the aim of an arms race, to achieve superiority over your enemy, is seldom gained or held for very long.

It is worth pointing out that one-third of the world's people are near or actually starving while some of the well-off countries spend billions of pounds on weapons of death. There is, however, no guarantee that if every penny spent on armaments was stopped tomorrow the money would then go to the most needy in the world.

It is also worth noting that within the countries of the big armaments spenders the money spent on weapons could be used to create jobs and help towards lowering the massive unemployment in the industrial countries of the world. It has been shown that the money spent on armaments does not create as many jobs as funds spent in other areas. The results of a study undertaken by the United States Bureau of Labour well illustrate this point. They compared figures of the number of jobs created for every one billion American dollars spent in various areas of industry, commerce and government.

Number of jobs created for every $1 billion spent

Military Spending	76 000
Engineering Industry	86 000
Government: Local and National	87 000
Transport Industries	92 000
Building Industry	100 000
Health Service	139 000
Education	187 000

(Source: US Bureau of Labour Figures, 1978.)

51

The point about military spending in all areas, not only nuclear, is that for it to be justified it must buy a country security. For it is the first duty of a government to try to provide security for its people against outside attack. Nuclear arms spending does not do this. There is no security against a nuclear attack.

> Every gun that is made; every warship that is launched; every rocket fired signifies a theft from those that hunger and are not fed, from those who are cold and are not clothed.
> (US President Eisenhower in the *New Internationalist,* March 1981.)

What Starts an Arms Race and What Keeps it Going?

1. *Action–Reaction*
Your enemies get a weapon which you believe makes them superior to you and so they could attack you and win or they could blackmail you until they get what they want. The obvious way out of this situation is for you to get the same weapon thereby putting yourself on equal terms with them. The enemies may react to this by producing a better weapon than the one they originally had.

The table that follows traces the action–reaction part of the arms race between the United States and the Soviet Union.

ACTION			REACTION	
USA	1945	Atomic bomb	USSR	1949
USA	1948	Long-range bomber	USSR	1955
USA	1954	Hydrogen bomb	USSR	1955
USSR	1957	ICBM	USA	1958
USSR	1957	First satellite in orbit	USA	1958

One-third of the world's population is starving while some countries spend billions of pounds on weapons of death

USA	1960	SLBM	USSR	1968
USA	1966	MRVed missiles	USSR	1968
USSR	1968	ABM	USA	1972
USA	1970	MIRVed missiles	USSR	1975
USA	1982	Cruise missile	USSR	1984?
USA	1983	Neutron bomb	USSR	198?
USA	199?	Killer-satellites	USSR	199?

Once this process gets underway it becomes very difficult to stop, as all arms races in history have shown. We have seen that without the will to disarm an arms race can go on and on. The nuclear arms race is like any other arms race with the major exception that it involves weapons of mass extermination.

Some nations claim that they are aiming for superiority over an enemy not to start a war or blackmail anyone, but to negotiate disarmament. They might say: 'Look, we are a lot bigger and better than you are so you had better start disarming along with us; or we will take steps to make you.'

This is called 'disarmament from strength'. There is no evidence in recent history to uphold this stand. The usual reaction of an inferior enemy is to try to build up their armaments or if they cannot do this then to search for friends to act with them and make them stronger.

2. Scientists and Technical 'Sweetness'

There would be no nuclear weapons without the contributions of scientists; they discovered the principles of the bomb and they obeyed instructions to produce the bomb. Scientists have been accused of being more interested in the technical problems of their projects; more concerned with producing technical perfection or 'sweetness' than with the consequences of their discoveries.

> Then Teller stood up and explained his new plan for a thermonuclear explosion illustrating it with figures on the blackboard. Now the attention of the scientists in the audience was riveted. They were carried away by the ingenuity of the idea ... 'It's cute,' exclaimed one scientist, 'it's beautifully cute!'
> (N. Moss, *Men Who Play God,* Penguin, 1968.)

> It is my judgement in these things that when you see something that is technically sweet, you go ahead and do it.
> (Robert Oppenheimer in N. Moss, op. cit.)

3. The Military–Industrial–Scientific Complex

When a politician gives the go-ahead for a project certain things must follow if that project is to achieve its aim.

The production of nuclear weapons and delivery systems needs money, knowledge, laboratories, factories, servicemen to use the weapons and people to administer the whole thing. Since 1945 a whole industry has grown up devoted to the design, production and deployment of nuclear weapons. Billions of pounds have been spent, thousands of jobs created. Many people's livelihoods, reputations and careers depend on nuclear weapons. Any threat to dismantle the nuclear weapons industry would be opposed by these people.

Once one project has finished another must start to keep them in work. They have gained an enormous influence over politicians because they are *the experts*; with their superior knowledge they can influence political decisions.

These people make up the Military–Industrial–Scientific Complex (MISC). They will involve themselves in *The 'What's Next' Process.*

4. The 'What's Next' Process

Very often weapons are designed and produced for which there is no purpose — the cruise missile programme went ahead before anyone had a clear idea of how the missile would be used.

The MISC is always searching for the 'what's next' weapon. For example, the Russians now say that they will develop their own cruise missile. The Americans then claim that they have to produce a newer and better cruise missile than the Russian one if they are to keep ahead.

The MISC have become modern-day prophets. They might say that in ten years' time the enemy could have developed a new superweapon; so they had better make it as well. And in ten years' time when the new weapon they wanted all along is available they can turn to the politicians and say, 'Look, we told you so.' They fulfil their own prophecies.

5. Political Rivalry

The most important reason for the present arms race is the rivalry between the United States and Soviet Union, without this there would be no nuclear arms race; their mutual distrust and dislike fuels the fires of the arms race. Nuclear weaponry is but one expression of their rivalry, but it is the most dangerous.

TASKS: Chapters 13 and 14

1. Is there anything that is so bad as to justify the use of nuclear weapons? Explain. Do you think everybody would think this thing was bad?
2. Your country has been attacked; all have been destroyed except you; what do you do? Launch a revenge attack on the enemy? Or do nothing? Why?
3. You may not be a Christian, you may be a Hindu, Muslim or Sikh or belong to some other religion. What does that religion teach about nuclear weapons? You might have no religion at all, but you will have views about what is right and wrong; how do you view nuclear weapons?
4. Disarming Outer Space

Two countries, A and B, *each* have the following deployed in space:

- 12 satellites armed with lasers; *purpose:* to destroy enemy nuclear missiles, in flight, before they reach their targets.
- 300 nuclear-armed orbiting space vehicles; *purpose:* to destroy the enemy's homeland if the enemy launches an attack first.
- 1 earth-orbiting space station; *purpose:* scientific research.
- 1 manned moon-base; *purpose:* scientific research.

These details are known to *both* countries.

It is the genuine intention of both countries to disarm space, but before they can negotiate with each other they have to prepare their proposals for the disarmament talks.

(i) Form two groups to represent country A and country B.

Each group should contain: a political leader, whose decisions on the negotiating proposals for the disarmament talks are final; a political adviser or advisers, who favour complete disarmament in space; and a military adviser or advisers, who are against complete disarmament in space.

Each group should work out, separately, its negotiating position as follows.

a) Decide some action which will show the other side that you genuinely desire to disarm.
b) Draw up a timetable for a gradual and phased disarmament process.

c) Decide the best method for verifying any actions that the other side may decide to take.

Remember that each group's political leader will have the final say on the negotiating positions.

(ii) Each country should now put its case to the other; the same roles as in part (i) can be used.

In the negotiations there is no one with a final say; no referee who can decide what each side must accept.

Agreement, if any, should be reached in stages; each stage must leave each side feeling secure. There must be some means agreed to verify each agreement.

Although you want to negotiate genuinely you do not trust the other side; somehow this mistrust must be overcome.

If you do not reach an agreement then that will not be surprising; if you do then perhaps the Americans and Russians could use you.

15   The USA versus the USSR

The developments in nuclear weaponry since 1945; the continuing arms race; the failure of arms control and disarmament negotiations to achieve any real breakthroughs can mostly be laid at the feet of these two countries.

What are their intentions? How do they see the world? How is it that two countries who fought a common enemy in Nazi Germany come to be deadly rivals today?

The USA — the Americans

America wants to go back to a time when movies were in black and white and so was everything else.
(Gil Heron, *Sanity*, June/July, 1982.)

The clock stood at four minutes to midday; the marshal could hear the distant sound of the clanking and puffing of the old steam engine as it neared the station; on board were the men who had sworn to kill him.

He waited for them alone. He could not run away. He knew they were bad; they had to be stopped. They could not be persuaded to go back. The marshal knew that this was more than just a gunfight in some dusty, little town in the American west.

He stood there ready to defend goodness, truth and decency against evil and lies. And he had to do it with his gun; it was the only language the men on the train understood.

All his friends had deserted him; even his wife had left town. They were all frightened of the men on the train; some had run away in search of safety; some

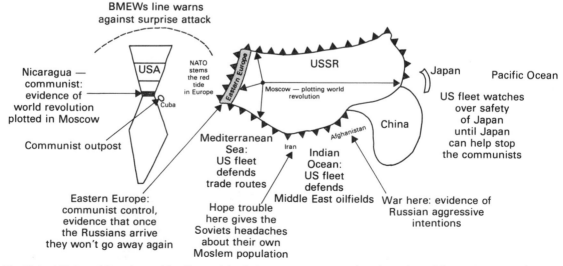

The United States of America making the world safe for democracy: one American view of the world

had remained ready to do a deal once the inevitable had happened and the bullet-ridden body of the marshal lay lifeless in the town's main street.

His friends had tried to persuade him to run away; to give in, but he knew that once he started to run nowhere would be safe. The men meant to kill him and they would pursue him to the ends of the earth to do so.

He would not try to do a deal with them. They were badmen and bullies. He knew that they would run his town to suit themselves and no one else. No; he had to stand there, gun in hand, and wait. No matter what the outcome he would live or die by what he knew was right.

The train, billowing clouds of steam, ground to a halt in the station. A few moments later the men got off, strapped their gunbelts round their hips and strode into town.

It was all over in a few minutes; the men were not quick enough or clever enough to beat the marshal. He had laid his plans carefully and although out-numbered he gunned them down. It was a triumph of good over evil.

(With grateful acknowledgements to *High Noon*.)

One way of understanding what the Americans believe they are like, in addition to books, is through western films. A good western will tell you a great deal about how Americans see themselves and their history. Often it is not what people really are like that dictates their actions, but what they *think* they are like.

The main things that emerge from an American western can be summed up as follows.

1. There is a clear dividing line between good and bad; there are no in-betweens; some people are 'goodies' and others are 'baddies'.
2. The goodies will always win provided they are constantly on their guard, because they have truth and decency and sometimes God on their side.
3. There are no genuine deals to be struck with the baddies; they would take this as a sign of weakness and demand more and more from you until they controlled you totally.
4. If your friends desert you because they are frightened or cannot see the justice of your cause you must fight on and never give in; you stand alone against the forces of evil.
5. You must be prepared to use violence against the baddies; this, in the end, is the only thing they understand; the only satisfactory way to deal with them.

Nowadays there are no baddies getting off trains to threaten all that is good. The villains for the Americans are the Communists, particularly the Russian Communists; evil, armed to the teeth and seeming to threaten the American way of life. The Communists are today's baddies and nuclear weapons have replaced the six-shooter.

It is sometimes said that the Americans are really British with different accents. The Europeans who first settled in any great numbers in what became the United States of America were British, mostly English. The American systems of government and law are based on the English systems; but there the similarity ends.

America became a great melting pot of nations. Massive numbers of immigrants went to the United States. They came from all corners of the earth, with the main groups being Africans (black slaves brought in to work the tobacco and cotton plantations), Irish, Italians, European Jews, Poles and Puerto Ricans, with smaller numbers coming from Germany, Scandinavia, Greece, Eastern Europe and many other places. A glance at a map of the United

States will show the different national groups by place names, or looking at the credits following an American TV programme or film will achieve the same thing.

To most immigrants America was billed as the land of opportunity and plenty; a land of freedom where an individual no matter how poor could succeed in making a decent, tolerant and prosperous life. This view gave rise to what is called the Great American Dream, which says that in America 'rags to riches' is possible in a land of plenty, rich in material goods and opportunity.

Most people went to America not only because they were poor or ambitious, but also to escape persecution in their home countries. America was the first British colony to achieve its freedom after fighting a war of independence.

Out of this experience other American beliefs arose:

a) dislike of dictatorship;
b) love of individual freedom; and
c) a belief that the American form of government — democracy — is the best in the world.

America became the land of hope; a land full of challenges to be met and overcome; a land of optimism and progress. Americans developed a belief that any problem can be solved with enough know-how and determination.

In the nineteenth and twentieth centuries America has been greatly influenced by the idea and reality of the 'frontier'. The frontier was the edge of civilisation beyond which the land lay untamed. In the last century the frontier moved steadily west at the expense of the Red Indians who were either killed or restricted to certain areas called reservations. The American pioneers through individual effort pushed the bounds of civilisation to the Pacific Ocean. In the twentieth century a new frontier has emerged — space travel — where the American pioneering spirit explores and delves with enthusiasm and energy.

America, by 1945, had become the most powerful nation on earth; a power built on the enormous natural wealth of the country and the energy of its people. Since 1945 American leaders by their words and actions have clearly reflected the experiences of American history as they see them. Constant themes are repeated:

● Democracy is good: Dictatorship is evil
● Truth, Justice, Individual Freedom are good: Persecution and Slavery are bad
● It is America's duty to fight against these evils.

It seems a very simple view of a very complicated world.

The USSR — the Russians

The distance from Berlin to Moscow is only 2000 kilometres. Yet 20 million Russians died to stop the Germans getting here. That is 10 000 dead Russians for every kilometre of road.
(Lt. General Victor Staradubov, the *Observer,* 11/4/84.)

Russia fears invasion from the West and with very good reason. There are no natural frontiers to hold up an invader, no sea, no mountain ranges, only the great, flat expanse of the North European Plain. In Britain we have no understanding of what an invasion is like; we have not been invaded since 1066. Yet in Russian history, invasions are common happenings and as time has gone by these invasions have had increasingly terrible consequences.

In the 1600s the Poles invaded Russia; in the early 1700s the Swedes; in 1812 Napoleon Bonaparte; in 1914 the Germans; in 1918/1919 the British, French, Americans and Japanese; in 1919 the Poles and in 1941 the Germans.

It is this latest invasion which will be remembered most by the Russians not only for its casualty figures — 20 million dead —

but also for its intention. A German victory would have meant the enslavement of the Russians and the settlement of their land by German colonists. Germany at the end of World War II was divided into an eastern and western part. Russians fear a re-united and re-armed Germany; particularly a Germany armed with nuclear weapons.

Since the defeat of Germany in 1945 the Russians have occupied and controlled most of the countries of Eastern Europe on which they have imposed Communist governments. These countries are used as a buffer zone against a future land attack from the West; any attack on these countries would probably cause a war.

The Russians are therefore obsessive about security; they have the largest country, by area, in the world with the longest land frontier to defend and they believe they are surrounded by real or potential enemies. In the West the United States with its soldiers and nuclear weaponry; the British and French with nuclear weapons; West Germany with the largest army in Western Europe. In the East a changeable China (the Soviet Union still possesses parts of the old Chinese Empire which it has never given back); Japan, a country not completely re-armed after its defeat in World War II, but nonetheless an American ally.

The Russian obsession with security has led them to be highly secretive. Their refusal to reveal precise figures about their armaments has led and is leading the United States and other countries to produce weaponry *in case* the Russians have them. Sometimes the Russians have claimed to have weapons they do not possess, which can only serve to fuel the continuing arms race. The need for secrecy felt by the Russians can reach ridiculous proportions when Russian-produced maps of the Soviet Union are falsified to show towns in the wrong places or in some cases whole towns which have 'disappeared'. Although spy-satellites have now given clearer and more accurate information about Russian military installations the obsession with secrecy, born from years of insecurity, still persists.

The Soviet Union not only fears outside attack, but also has problems within its borders with minority groups. Although they form over half of its people the Russians are one national group among many in the Soviet Union.

The Soviet Union is what we call a Communist country; although the Russians and other Communists refer to their countries as 'socialist' ones that are 'building Communism'.

What is Communism? Why is it feared by Western countries?

Today Communism is associated with many unpleasant and terrible things such

'Never, but never again.'

59

as police States, prison camps and dictatorships. However, the idea of Communism is as old as human society.

Communism means a perfect world; a world without want or war; a world of peace where people's energies are directed into building a decent and prosperous life for everyone. Another name for Communism is Utopia: the perfect world. The ideas of Communism are very attractive to people searching for a way out of oppression or persecution or need.

Modern ideas of how Communism is to be arrived at are based on the writings of a German who lived in the nineteenth century — Karl Marx. His writings are usually referred to as Marxism.

Marxism tells the story of human beings; their history, their present condition and their future. History is usually portrayed as the story of the actions of individuals: good kings and bad kings; heroes, heroines and villains. Marxism looks at history in a totally different way. Although it does not deny the importance of individuals it says that what really matters in history are the actions of groups of people called 'classes'.

Marxism pointed out that history can be seen as the story of how a minority of people has possessed more power and wealth than the majority in any one country. It is true that in most countries a minority of people do have more than the majority; there are rich people and there are poor people; the 'haves' and the 'have-nots'.

Marxism says that the rich are not rich because they deserve to be nor the poor needy because they deserve to be. The rich stay wealthy because they use their power to make sure that things stay that way; they control the police and the armed forces; they write the law of the land to suit themselves. Throughout history there have always been classes of people; a minority has controlled a majority; a minority has been richer than the rest. In the Middle Ages there were lords and their serfs and in

modern times the ruling minority are called the capitalists or bourgeoisie and the ruled majority the proletariat or working class.

Marxism tells how the working class can take power and wealth away from the capitalists and distribute it among themselves; it is a recipe for revolution. Communists see most countries in the West such as ourselves, the Americans, the French and others as capitalist countries. The ruling groups of the capitalist countries, therefore, have good reason to fear Marxism because it tells of their downfall and they have every reason to prevent its spread.

Marx did not simply put a new slant on history; he turned it into a science. A science with laws, just as chemistry or physics has laws. Marx claimed his science of history could predict the future of human society. The future could be foretold by understanding the way the laws of history had acted in the past. On this basis the capitalists would eventually be overthrown, usually by a revolution, and the working class would take over and then run the world. They would be led by the Communist Party which would build socialism, which is seen as the half-way stage to the perfect world — Communism.

Communism's progress throughout the world is *inevitable* said Marx; it must happen; it cannot be stopped. The actions of individuals can either quicken or slow down its spread, but it can never be halted.

Marx's view of the world has not proved to be totally correct, in fact a lot of it has proved to be completely untrue. However, its message of hope for the poor and downtrodden remains just as strong as ever; and Marxists control not only the largest country in the world, Russia, but also the country with the largest population, China, and many others.

Earlier we mentioned the Russian obsession with security. In Marxism there is equally a worry about security. Marx supposed that the Communist Party would lead and win revolutions in all the highly-industrialised countries of the world such as Britain, America and Germany. The industrialised countries were militarily the strongest in the world and so the Communist parties in these countries would feel secure from attack by the weaker non-Communist world. The spread of Communism could then go ahead on a secure base.

The idea that Communism could survive alone in one country or that Communism could grow in a backward agricultural land was not considered either practical or possible; and yet this is exactly what happened.

In 1917, Russia, a backward agricultural country with a very small working class became the scene of the first Communist revolution. The Communist Party in Russia expected revolutions to occur almost at once in Germany, America and Britain. This did not happen and they were left to stand on their own. It is a belief of Communists that they will inevitably be attacked by capitalist countries. In the case of Russia this is just what did happen in 1919, and 1941.

Russians fear attack from the West; Communists know the capitalists will attack them; therefore a Russian who is also a Communist must feel a *double insecurity.* The Russian Communists see the United States as the leading capitalist country and therefore their main enemy; most other capitalist countries, such as Britain, are viewed as satellites of the United States.

Since 1917 the actions of the Soviet leadership have been mainly cautious and defensive and very often slow in world affairs. They have used armed force to protect their border on a number of occasions, Hungary in 1956, Czechoslovakia in 1968 and Afghanistan in 1979. Generally speaking they have not been rash or impetuous outside these areas except on one notable occasion in 1962 when their involvement with Cuba brought the world close to its third and probably final war.

The Cold War

Since 1945 the relationship between the United States and the Soviet Union has been so full of distrust and dislike that it has been called the Cold War. Although there have been times when the Cold War has eased up, such as the late 1950s and early 1970s, the rivalry of these two countries has remained as strong as ever.

Russia and America emerged from World War II as the most powerful countries on earth; they had different ways of life and different views of the world. Their relationship has dominated the world into which you were born. They have most of the world's nuclear weapons and so what they have done, are doing and will do is of the greatest importance.

The Americans have a clear and simple view of what the Russians are after:

> . . . world domination. It's just that simple.
> (Caspar Weinberger, US Defense Secretary, April 1984.)

The US President, Ronald Reagan referred to the Soviet Union as:

> . . . the focus of evil in the modern world.
> . . . the sinful empire.
> (*The Observer,* 24/4/83.)

The Russians have expressed similar sentiments towards the capitalists in the West:

> We will bury you.
> Your grandchildren will live under Communism.
> (Nikita Khrushchev, Soviet leader, 1953–64.)

The United States believes the Soviet Union is out to dominate the world. The Soviet Union believes that the United States is out to dominate the world. Events since 1945 can be used to justify either or both of these statements.

For a short period after 1945 the Americans talked about 'rolling-back' the frontiers of Communism, which meant a threat to remove the Communist governments which ruled in Eastern Europe. However, this talk soon stopped as it was obvious that any attempt to do this would provoke a world war because the Russians regarded control of Eastern Europe as essential to their security.

In March 1947, the United States announced that instead of rolling-back Communism it would 'contain' it. The containment of Communism meant that the United States would not allow the Soviet Union to control areas other than those they held in 1947. The Americans followed up this statement with attempts to form alliance systems which would effectively surround the Soviet Union. By the middle 1950s, at enormous cost, they had largely succeeded in doing so.

The most important of these alliances was the North Atlantic Treaty Organisation

(NATO), formed in April 1949. The official reason for its formation is given as follows:

> Britain, America and Russia had been allies in the Second World War. However, almost immediately after the war in Europe ended distrust grew between Russia and her other wartime allies. There were many complex reasons for this. It is, however, a fact that after the war Russia directly or indirectly forced Eastern European countries to adopt Communist governments. As a result the Western European countries, with America and Canada, came to believe that their individual security was threatened by Russia. They considered that unless they did something about it one country after another in Western Europe might be taken over by the Russians. Their best course they believed was to band together in the NATO alliance for collective protection.
> (NATO: Defence Fact Sheet 2 Ministry of Defence, London, 1981.)

Eventually the North Atlantic Treaty was signed by Britain, America, Canada, France, Holland, Belgium, Luxembourg, Denmark, Iceland, Italy, Norway, Portugal, Greece,

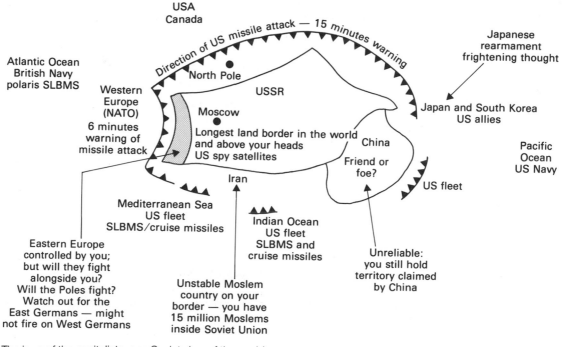

The jaws of the capitalists: one Soviet view of the world

Turkey, West Germany and Spain. France opted out of the military aspects of NATO and conducts an independent defence policy.

The Americans dominate NATO; its chief is always an American serviceman. The Russians see NATO as a direct threat to them and a clear example of tight American control over its West European satellite States. The Treaty states that an attack by anyone on one of its member States will be regarded as an attack against them all. From the European point of view this commits the United States to defend Europe in case of war.

In response to the formation and threat posed by NATO the Russians collected their satellite States together and formed the Warsaw Pact in 1955. It includes the Soviet Union, Bulgaria, Czechoslovakia, the German Democratic Republic (East Germany), Hungary, Poland and Romania.

You may hear public mention of NATO forces or NATO conferences or Warsaw Pact manoeuvres; remember that these names really mean America and Russia; they are the labels for their rivalry in Europe.

The Americans believe in the 'domino theory' of Communism which states that if one country falls to the Communists its neighbours might fall next. The domino theory partly provoked the formation of NATO. America can show that this idea has a certain element of truth to it, for after the formation of NATO other countries outside Europe fell to the Communists: China, in 1949, being the major example of this.

Another American belief was that every Communist movement in the world was controlled by the Russians. This has been shown not to be true. What usually happened was that Communist or nationalist movements turned to the Russians for help against the governments they were fighting.

The problem with the containment of Communism is that military bases do not stop the spread of ideas; a bullet cannot kill the power of a thought. Since 1947 Communism has spread beyond the lines laid down by the Americans' original statement; it now exists in Vietnam, Laos, China, Cuba, Nicaragua and parts of the Middle East and Africa. However, its spread has been due more to terrible oppression and poverty than any manipulation by the Russians and where Communism does exist outside Russia and most of Eastern Europe it has adapted itself to suit domestic circumstances. In a sense there is no longer such a thing as Communism but a list of differing versions of national Communism. Chinese Communism is not the same as Russian Communism; even in Eastern Europe differences are to be found, Polish Communism is not the same model as Hungarian Communism.

However, all Communists no matter what their national differences still believe that they have one common enemy — the capitalist countries of the world. And the capitalist countries no matter what their national differences still believe that they have one common enemy — the Communist countries of the world.

The existence of nuclear weapons in a world full of rivalry, distrust and hatred can have two effects, (a) to hasten the end of civilisation as we understand it or (b) because of their dreadful destructive potential, prevent another world war. Those who favour the retention of nuclear weapons or at least accept the idea that we have to live with them can point to the Cuban Missile Crisis of October 1962, to give credibility to their arguments.

The Cuban Missile Crisis proved to be one of the most important events of the Cold War. We said earlier that the Soviet leadership has usually been cautious in its actions, but when opportunities to embarrass or blackmail their enemies have arisen without any real fear of retaliation these opportunities have been taken. Cuba was one example of this which went badly wrong for them.

Cuba lies in the Carribean Sea 90 miles from Miami Beach, Florida, USA. In 1959 a young Marxist lawyer named Fidel Castro led a revolution which replaced an American-sponsored dictator. Cuba was important to the United States: as well as providing cheap sugar for the American market, it was well outside the limits laid down by the Americans for the containment of Communism.

Soon after Castro came to power plans were laid by the Americans for his removal. Acting on information that the Cuban people would rise and overthrow Castro if given an excuse the Americans organised an invasion force which landed at the Bay of Pigs in Cuba in April 1961. It was a total failure; the people did not rise; the Cuban exiles used by the Americans as the invasion force were either captured or slaughtered on the beaches.

The world waited for the inevitable; a full-scale American invasion of Cuba; it was expected by everyone — Castro, the Russians, the American people. No American government had stood idly by and let regimes hostile to it survive for very long in the Carribean or Central America.

Nothing happened; no preparations for an invasion; no invasion.

The Russian leader, Khrushchev, con-cluded only one thing from all this; that the American President, Kennedy, was a weak man; a man frightened to act boldly. In June 1961, Kennedy and Khrushchev met for talks in Vienna, Austria. Khrushchev's original view of Kennedy was confirmed.

The Russians saw the opportunity to deal a blow to American self-respect and prestige. For years the Russians had experienced the threat posed by American bases on or near their borders; now here was a chance to do the same to the Americans.

Khrushchev seems to have hoped to wreck American credibility as an ally of the countries of Western Europe and harm American status throughout Central and South America. For if Kennedy did nothing about a Communist country 90 miles from America what hope was there for American promises to defend Western Europe, 3000 miles from home?

Khrushchev, without Castro's knowledge, started to ship nuclear missiles to Cuba; if they could be set up and operational then Khrushchev hoped to blackmail the United States over various issues, such as American bases in Europe. Khrushchev had made an enormous blunder; Kennedy had, in fact, not invaded Cuba because it was obvious that the Cuban people supported Castro and any American invasion would involve a lengthy and costly campaign. In addition, the Americans' declared aim to support people fighting for their freedom from oppression would look very silly and hypocritical if they attacked a country whose people clearly supported their own government.

An American U-2 spyplane, overflying and photographing Cuba in October 1962, brought back film which showed clear evidence of the construction of Russian land-based ballistic missile launch-pads. Without alerting their allies in Europe the Americans moved quickly. Cuba was surrounded by warships; and the Russians, taken by surprise, were told that any ship that tried to break through the American blockade would be stopped, searched and perhaps turned back. There was a Russian convoy carrying missiles heading for Cuba at the time. Also the Americans told the Russians to dismantle their missile sites in Cuba and remove them. The United States made it clear that failure to obey would mean war.

The scene was now set for the international version of the game of 'chicken'. Chicken was usually played by young people in America. Two cars would travel at high speed down a road directly at each other. If neither driver swerved they would crash head-on and both be killed; if someone at the last moment swerved to avoid a crash they would be seen as cowards for having 'chickened out'. International chicken has been played many times in history not with cars but with whole armies and in the case of Cuba with the fate of the world at stake.

In response to American demands the Russians started the game of chicken; they ordered their convoy on route to Cuba to continue and increase its speed. Soviet submarines were despatched to the Carribean Sea. The Americans reacted by placing their armed forces throughout the world on full alert. The Russians responded by demanding that the Americans remove their ballistic missiles from Turkey, which bordered the Soviet Union.

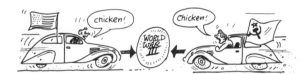

The tension built to such an extent that the Americans thought war was inevitable. It is not clear what happened in Moscow, but it seems that Khrushchev was forced to realise that he had made an enormous mistake; he had read Kennedy wrongly.

It was the Russians who ended the game; they chickened out. The convoy was halted, the missiles dismantled and removed. However, the Americans realised that the game of chicken involves total humiliation for the loser; the loser is seen to be a coward. In the Cuban crisis the Russians were not humiliated because such an enemy might strike back to save face or honour. The Americans avoided this

situation by promising the Russians that in the future Cuba would not be invaded by them. So the Russians could at least claim that they had achieved something from the crisis.

The main effects of the Cuban Missile Crisis can be summed up as follows.

1. The United States and the Soviet Union have ever since avoided direct confrontations realising that these situations could lead to nuclear war.
2. They improved communications between each other through the installation of the hotline between Washington and Moscow so that in times of crisis misunderstandings could be avoided.
3. The lesson learned by Europe was that at times of crisis neither of the big powers would really bother consulting their allies. The big people would settle their disputes without reference to the little people.
4. It can be claimed that it was fear of nuclear war that made the Russians chicken out and so possession of nuclear weapons actually prevented a new war.

The Cold War — An Alternative Version

The Americans want to dominate the world. The Russians want to dominate the world. These simple statements are used to explain why huge sums of money have to be spent on armaments; why these armaments have to be constantly modernised.

The Americans tell their own people and the peoples of Western Europe that the Cold War is due solely to Russian aggressive intentions.

The Russians tell their own people and the peoples of Eastern Europe that the Cold War is due solely to American aggressive intentions.

What is the truth?

There is another version of the Cold War which explains its causes in a very different way; this runs as follows.

Suppose you are part of a large, although unusual, family; brothers, sisters, mothers, fathers, cousins, uncles, aunts and grandparents. The family is run by a small group called 'Heads of the Household' or for short, H of H.

The H of H have the best of everything; the best food; the best beds; the best clothes. Naturally the H of H do not want these things taken away from them; they like things just the way they are.

They tell you not to grumble about this; you are better off than your parents and grandparents were; you have more than the people down the road and anyway things will get much better in the future. The H of H explain that they get the best of everything because they deserve to; they have to deal with all the problems of running a large family and you do not. They say that if you do not cause trouble you might one day be a member of the H of H group and have all the good things for yourself.

The H of H hold late night meetings after everybody else has gone to bed; you are curious to know what they talk about.

The meeting was well underway as you crouched down at the door and listened. They were talking about squabbles within the family and what to do about them. You heard familiar names mentioned — Stuart is a troublemaker, Dawn is a gossip — but they reserved the really harsh words for your cousin, Pete.

One of the group said Pete had always been a problem, right from birth; never co-operative, questioned every order, stayed out late. He mixed with the wrong sort of people. But his latest crime was the worst of all because he has been going round the other known troublemakers and hold-ing meetings with them. Someone had obviously told the H of H what went on at these meetings because one of them had a note pad with all the information on it.

Pete had been telling the others that it was about time that the H of H group was replaced. Why should they have the best of everything while the rest had to make do with leftovers? Worse than this, Pete seemed to have won over some members of the family who had never been known as troublemakers before; his influence seemed to be spreading.

The H of H listened to all this and then their leader, old Uncle Cyril, spoke.

'We all know that if we are to stay as Heads of the Household we must have the obedience of those beneath us; they must do as they are told; they must respect us and look up to us. It's what I like to call family togetherness, it sounds more friendly than obedience.'

Several voices then came into the discussion.

'Pete is a problem; I've promised him extra pocket-money if he's good, but it doesn't seem to make any difference.'

'I'd send him away.'

'No,' said Uncle Cyril, 'that wouldn't solve anything; someone else would take his place as chief troublemaker.'

'Wouldn't it be easier if we shared out all we've got with the rest of the family.' It was Uncle Ken.

A deathly hush descended on the meeting, Uncle Cyril got up and said solemnly and quietly: 'Are you mad? We will never do that; we are going to have to use Plan C again; it never fails. We have used it before; it's the quickest and best method I know to sort out family quarrels and troublemakers.'

Everyone at the meeting seemed to know what Plan C was; and by the next day Plan C was well underway.

The following morning Uncle Cyril and the rest of the H of H group called a meeting of the whole family. Uncle Cyril rose to address everyone, flanked by his main

compete with American economic control. Japan, which never invested a great deal in armaments after the war, began to expand into American and European markets. Recently America has been trying to persuade the Japanese to divert more money to armaments using the threat of Soviet power in the Far East to do this.

This version says the real threat to American economic and political stability is an expansion of European and Japanese economic might in the world and not a cautious, security-conscious, economically relatively powerless Russia.

Are we therefore threatened with extinction by nuclear destruction simply because small groups of people in America and Russia want to keep their privileged positions?

TASK: Chapter 15

There are three main reasons given for the continuing Cold War:

a) a straightforward struggle between the USA and USSR;

b) a contrived Cold War to ensure the ruling groups in Russia and America keep their privileges; and

c) an American device to keep down the economic and political threat that a revived Europe could pose to American dominance of the Western world.

Which version is true? And why? Or are they all true?

16   Nuclear deterrence and beyond

Nuclear weapons are often referred to as a 'deterrent' to war. What does this mean?

Imagine you have enemies; you believe they would, given the chance, attack and kill you. You know that they fear you, just as much as you fear them. How are you going to stop them from attacking you?

One way is to *deter* them; which means making them *believe* that if they attack you then you can damage them just as much as they can damage you. You must convince them that the result of such an attack could end in their total destruction.

This is the situation that has existed between the United States and the Soviet Union since the early 1950s. Neither side will attack the other with nuclear weapons because the consequence of doing so is mutually assured destruction (MAD). Why launch your bombers and missiles to destroy the other side if you know that in return they will blow you off the face of the earth?

This seems a safe enough assumption to make; and we can look back over the past thirty years and claim that nuclear weapons, acting as a deterrent, have prevented the suspicion and mistrust between the United States and the Soviet Union from erupting into World War III. We can point, as we have seen, to the Cuban Missile Crisis, which was the only occasion when the United States and the Soviet Union confronted each other directly, and say that a war between them was prevented because the Soviet leadership became convinced that the United States would use its nuclear weapons in a conflict. It is claimed by some that this was an example of nuclear weapons making a positive contribution to peace; and that ever since that time the Superpowers have avoided any further face-to-face situations and so made the possibility of another world war recede.

However, we must put forward the other side of the argument and mention the dangers surrounding the reality of nuclear deterrence. Return, for the moment, to your imaginary enemies; what could go wrong with your deterrence of each other?

Major Dangers of Nuclear Deterrence

1. *The Madman Situation*
Suppose your enemies are lunatics, determined to destroy you despite the consequences to themselves. All your sane and sensible arguments about 'if you hit me, I'll hit you' might have no effect whatsoever.

Would nuclear deterrence have worked with Adolf Hitler in his last desperate days in the Berlin bunker in April 1945? What are the chances of another Hitler coming to power, this time with a finger on a nuclear firing button?

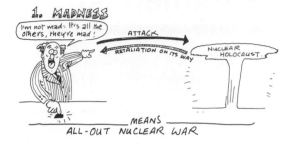

2. *The 'Let's-Get-On-With-It' Situation*
There are times, in highly tense situations, when you may act impulsively because you have reached the limits of your tolerance.

Before the Soviet Union possessed nuclear weapons and the United States had a monopoly on them some American politicians and soldiers foresaw the dangers of living on the knife-edge which Soviet acquisition of nuclear weapons would bring about. Their solutions to the problem varied from the suggestion that the United States abandon its nuclear weapons and thereby persuade the Soviet Union not to acquire them; to the opposite extreme of wiping out the Russians before it was too late.

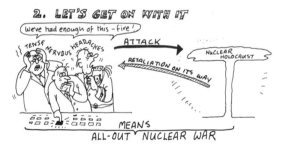

The world has lived under the threat of nuclear weapons for over thirty years and some commentators fear that eventually the strain will tell on politicians or soldiers and the urge to 'get-on-with-it' may become too great to withstand any longer.

3. *Accidental War*
Your enemies stand in front of you; their backs to the sun; the light makes it difficult for you to see them clearly. You think you see an arm move towards you.

Are they going to attack you? They are your *enemies*; you cannot take the chance that their arm movements are innocent gestures. You attack!

A nuclear missile takes under thirty minutes to travel between the United States and the Soviet Union. This does not leave a great deal of time to check whether an alert is real or not. The enormous speed of missiles makes cool, calm thinking almost impossible.

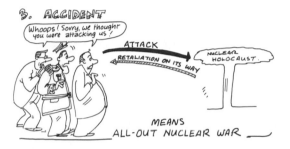

The whole of the American and Soviet nuclear war machine is totally computerised; they rely entirely on machines to warn them of an attack. We do not really know how many times both countries have come to a full nuclear alert because of a computer failure or the inability of radar scanners to distinguish between a flight of migrating geese and a hail of missiles.

But rather like you having to decide whether your enemies' arm movement is accidental or not, so Americans and Russians have to make equally rapid decisions under pressure.

So far they have made the right ones.

4. *Miscalculation*
As we noted earlier, deterrence depends on making your enemies believe you will attack them if they attack you; this is called making your deterrent *credible*.

There is no question that the Soviet Union and the United States have sufficient nuclear weapons to destroy each other many times over; their deterrents are certainly credible in this sense. No one is in any doubt that massive destruction can be a reality.

But deterrence is to do with belief; your enemies are well-armed, but does it follow that they will actually use their weapons? Do you suspect that when it comes to the crunch they may back down?

This was the situation which launched the Cuban Missile Crisis. The Soviet leader, Khrushchev, having met the American President, Kennedy, concluded that here was a weak-willed man, a man who could be manipulated and threatened without the fear of retaliation. This turned out to be an enormous miscalculation by Khrushchev because Kennedy was prepared to use nuclear weapons. Fortunately Khrushchev realised his miscalculation before it was too late and backed away from the confrontation with Kennedy.

Misreading or miscalculating an enemy's intentions has been the cause of many wars in our history; it is still a very real and dangerous problem in the nuclear age.

5. *The Breakthrough Fear*

If your enemies are people who would be satisfied with threatening you with a punch on the nose (if they got the chance), then at least you would know what to expect. You could prepare quietly and efficiently for such an eventuality by perhaps wearing a cricketer's helmet with a face visor. You would know that if they did hit you they would bruise their knuckles and you might feel some unpleasant vibrations around your head.

Unfortunately they are not like that. They are adventurous; for ever searching for new and more fiendish ways of attacking you. You never know from one day to the next what new weapon they might try to use against you.

Perhaps they will appear with a sledge-hammer and threaten to smash your helmet to bits. You guard against this by buying a crossbow to keep them at a distance. In the meantime, however, they have bought a high-velocity rifle, making your crossbow totally ineffective.

You have both spent, and are still spending, a great deal of time, energy and money in looking for a lasting advantage over each other; something you have yet to find. This, as we have seen, is called an arms race.

The weapons of nuclear deterrence are not things which remain the same. The weapons of thirty years ago are not those of today. The sub-sonic bomber has given way to the Intercontinental Ballistic Missile.

The reliability and stability of nuclear deterrence depends on *certain* knowledge of your enemy's capabilities. When these are constantly changing deterrence can become unstable.

If your enemies do get one step ahead of you, might they not be tempted to use any new breakthrough to attack you before you can catch up with them?

So far we have examined nuclear deterrence and the possible ways it could fail. We now go on to discuss the ways in which nuclear weapons could be used in a war.

NATO has plans for the possible course of war against the Soviet Union; nuclear weapons figure largely in these plans. We will see how NATO views events after nuclear deterrence has failed.

World War III
(NATO version)

An incident somewhere in the world has brought the Soviet Union and NATO to a face-to-face confrontation in Europe. Neither side backs down. The Russians attack and their tanks move across Germany. NATO's forces, weak and outnumbered, cannot stem the attack by ordinary or conventional weapons.

The Supreme Allied Commander in Europe is empowered to use nuclear weapons against the advancing Soviet army. He does so.

The Soviets, in return, launch a nuclear strike against NATO's forces, which includes all military and communication facilities in Western Europe and Britain.

The United States, committed by the NATO treaty to defend Europe and prevent its occupation by the Soviet Union, launches a massive nuclear attack on Russia. In retaliation, the Russians launch an equally massive attack on the United States.

The breakdown of nuclear deterrence will bring an end to civilisation as we know it.

The full horror of this situation is portrayed very clearly by NATO in order to strengthen nuclear deterrence. Deterrence *must work*, because look what would happen if it did not! It can be said that one of the strengths of nuclear deterrence lies in a knowledge of the full horror of the consequences of its failure.

This version of the results of the collapse of deterrence is still the official NATO view, but events which have been happening recently have steadily undermined the official view and in the 1980s deterrence may well be abandoned.

Why should this be so?

As we have seen, the American commitment to defend Europe could lead, in the end, to a massive nuclear attack on the United States itself. Some American military thinkers have, for many years, argued that there are ways of avoiding such a catastrophe whilst still keeping the pledge to defend Europe.

Recently, such phrases as 'flexible response', 'limited nuclear war', 'protracted nuclear war' and 'first-strike winnable nuclear war' have been talked about publicly. All these seemingly bewildering phrases are different varieties of nuclear warfare which, if successfully fought, would avoid a direct, all-out Soviet attack on the United States. Let us examine each one of them and see what they mean.

1. *Flexible Response*
You are again facing your enemies knowing that if deterrence fails you will either give in to them or quickly fight it out to the death.

When you consider this situation doesn't it all seem rather silly, childish and perhaps unnecessary? Surely you do not have to fight to a sudden death finish if deterrence breaks down? You want to stay alive and so do they. There must be a way of persuading them that in an all-out war no one will win.

You could, of course, agree to disarm instantly and shake hands, but you do not trust each other enough for that. What else can you do short of an all-out attack?

Suppose deterrence has failed and conflict is about to happen; instead of a massive attack on your enemies you could merely kick them on the shins. They are bruised and hurt, but they will not die. You have shown them you mean business! They

72

F-4E Phantom II aircraft

have had the warning to come no further. If they ignore this warning and still advance you could break their legs in an attempt to disable them.

Gradually increasing the variety and violence of your reactions to an enemy attack is called flexible response. NATO now possesses the weaponry for a flexible response to a Russian attack. In the 1950s such a response would have been impossible because most nuclear weapons were carried aboard aeroplanes sited at bases throughout the world and intended for a massive and speedy destruction of Soviet cities. However, over the years other nuclear weapons have appeared; these are small in explosive yield and can be fired by field guns, just as ordinary shells can be

Men of 50 Missile Regiment preparing Lance

fired. NATO possesses many hundreds of pieces of this so-called nuclear artillery. In addition missiles now exist with ranges of a few hundred miles or less. These, as we have seen, are called tactical nuclear weapons.

The purpose of these weapons is to inflict damage over a relatively small area; they are meant to be the 'kick on the shins' to advancing Soviet forces. They are the first stage of a flexible response to an attack. The latest proposed addition to NATO's nuclear armoury, the neutron bomb, is meant to fit into this picture of a flexible nuclear response.

Military thinkers have realised that a flexible response must involve planning for other actions as well as the use of tactical

M 109 155mm Self-propelled Howitzer

nuclear weapons. Some suggest a long-range attack might take place on a Russian city.

The advantage of a flexible response is that it gives both sides time to think clearly what they are doing and hopefully stop their attacks.

There are two major disadvantages.

a) It could signal to enemies that your threats of all-out destruction, if deterrence fails, are not really serious. If you mean to destroy them completely in the end, why bother with a flexible response? What may seem a sensible position from NATO's point of view could be read as a sign of weakness by them.

b) Flexible response assumes that once a war begins each action taken in the fighting will be tightly controlled by the chief commanders of the armed forces. But would this really happen in the heat of battle? Would emotions rather than clear thinking rule actions?

    The history of previous wars shows that battles can be won or lost by unplanned actions taken by individual fighting units on the spur of the moment.

    We also know that communications between soldiers and their leaders could be severely disrupted by the effects of the electromagnetic pulse (EMP).

Once the first nuclear weapon is used we have crossed the *nuclear threshold.* We step into a whole new area of war. We know a good deal about conventional or non-nuclear war and its weaponry; about the stresses felt by soldiers and their commanders; but we have never had the experience of a nuclear war.

It can be claimed that once the nuclear threshold is crossed, as a part of a flexible response, things would soon get out of hand and an all-out long-range attack would quickly follow.

2. Limited Nuclear War

The idea that a nuclear war can be limited geographically is now receiving some prominence in American thinking. At the moment the limited geographical area is taken to mean Europe, including Britain. The reason for this is that Europe is assumed to be the place where nuclear weapons will be used first as a part of a flexible response to an attack.

It is said that once tactical nuclear weapons are used in Europe such will be the horror and revulsion at the destruction caused that the Americans and Russians will

F-111 aircraft

pull back from an all-out attack on each other.

3. *Protracted Nuclear War*

This states that a nuclear war can be fought, not over a few hours or days, but could be sustained for months with each side carefully selecting targets which they hope will sap the enemy's resolve to fight on. Protracted nuclear war is not limited geographically; targets would range all over the world. These targets could include cities, military targets and communication centres.

Protracted nuclear war can be compared with two boxers fighting it out over fifteen rounds; each one hoping the other will throw in the towel.

"Boy, are we lucky it was only a LIMITED nuclear war!"

Alas Poor Europe I Knew Her Well

4. *First-strike Winnable Nuclear War*

Under nuclear deterrence the idea that anyone could win a nuclear war is considered complete nonsense. For the first time in history nuclear weapons had created a situation where no one could win; everyone would be a loser; there would be no victors; destruction was mutually assured.

Neither the United States nor the Soviet Union would attack each other first because they could not be sure of destroying the other side's missiles. It would be complete madness to attack your enemies because they could strike back and destroy you.

However, suppose that through advances in technology it became possible to think of hitting the other side *first* and destroying sufficient of their missiles to make an effective retaliation impossible. Wouldn't that make the idea of winning a nuclear war a real possibility?

This is exactly what is happening now. Return again to your enemies; you are face-to-face; you all have guns. Deterrence is in operation, because you will not fire first as you believe that they have a chance of firing back and killing you.

Suppose that some of your friends have been working feverishly for many months on some method of destroying not your enemies but their *guns,* before they have a chance to fire them.

At last, your friends achieve the great breakthrough, a gun is placed in your hand, the bullets from which are so accurate that they cannot fail to knock the gun out of your enemies' hands *before* they can pull their own triggers. You can now strike first and win; for without their guns your enemies are, at last, at your mercy.

One of the most significant advances in nuclear weapons technology of the past twenty years has been the increasing accuracy of missiles. We are now talking of hitting targets thousands of miles away with accuracies of within 90 feet of these targets.

Breakthroughs in technology are at the point of making nuclear deterrence a thing of the past. Land-based missiles are no longer safe in their underground silos. Direct hits on them will destroy them where they stand; they will be useless for retaliation.

In addition to accuracy one missile, as we have seen, is claimed to be *undetectable* by radar — the cruise missile.

There remains only one area where a nuclear deterrent is safe, at least for the time-being, and that is under the sea on board nuclear submarines. Although even here, the Americans claim that they are on the verge of perfecting a system of anti-submarine warfare which will track and destroy enemy submarines with assured success.

The idea of a winnable nuclear war, once just a military thinker's dream, now seems to be a real possibility.

A Further Note on Limited War and First-Strike Capability

The whole nuclear arsenal of the United States is undergoing modernisation. The

updating takes the form mainly of making missiles, either highly accurate, undetectable by present day radar systems, or both.

As we have seen the cruise missile (now in Britain at Greenham Common) is accurate and supposedly undetectable. Another new missile, the Pershing II, being installed in Europe is also highly accurate. Of these two it is Pershing which alarms the Russians more, not only because it is accurate and therefore capable of pinpoint destruction of their missiles and military command centres, but also because it gives them only six minutes warning of its approach.

We have seen how important 'think-time' is with nuclear weapons. Six minutes does not give the Russians a lot of time to decide if their radar is playing them false or if the air is really thick with missiles. The Russians have responded to the threat posed by Pershing II with a 'launch-on-warning' policy, which means that they will not bother to check up whether there are really missiles coming at them, they will launch their own missiles on warning; with only six minutes to decide they must plan for the worst possible situation.

The reason given by the United States for developing highly accurate weapons that could be used to strike first at Russian missiles with a hope of winning a nuclear war is,

> they (the Russians) are designing their weapons in such a way and in sufficient numbers to indicate to us that they think they could begin and win a nuclear war.
> (Caspar Weinberger, US Defense Secretary, August 1982.)

So it seems obvious that the United States would have to do the same thing, that is, make weapons that could win a nuclear war. However, the Americans deny that this is the reason for their production.

> We must have a capability for a survivable and endurable response to demonstrate that . . . our forces could survive Soviet strikes over an extended period. Thus we believe we could *deter* [author's emphasis] any attack.
> (Weinberger, op.cit.)

The United States claims that its new weapons are meant to *deter* a Russian attack because it believes it is the Russians who want to start a nuclear war and so the American deterrent must be modernised to survive a Soviet attack.

As we have seen most American warheads are safe from attack on board submarines deep in the oceans of the world with sufficient power to devastate the Soviet Union.

Therefore the American reason for modernisation still does not answer the question — why accuracy? The other side can be deterred from attacking by the threat that their people will be wiped out; high levels of accuracy are not needed for this.

The Russian commander of the Warsaw Pact forces responded to the American modernisation plans by claiming that the United States was preparing for another world war and counting on victory.

On the idea of limiting a nuclear war to Europe and sparing America the Soviet Defence Minister, Marshal Ustinov said,

> . . . if they think in Washington that we will retaliate only against targets in Western Europe they badly delude themselves. Retaliation against the United States will be ineluctable.*
> (Ustinov, April 1983.)

The Americans claim that modernisation of their forces is solely to improve their deterrent capacity and yet there are contradictions to this.

> From the outset it is acknowledged that . . . it would be advantageous to use tactical nuclear . . . weapons at an early stage and in enemy territory. Theatre forces should not be considered solely as a bridge to (all-out) nuclear war. They are weapons which must be

---

*Ineluctable means something against which it would be useless to struggle. The Russians do not believe that nuclear war can be limited.

considered in the context of a *war-fighting* [author's emphasis] capability.
(Source: US Army and Air Force document *Joint Attack of the 2nd Echelon,* 1982.)

Weapons now exist with such levels of accuracy that they could destroy missiles and command centres and so make the possibility of a winnable nuclear war more real.

Both the Russians and Americans have first-strike weapons which they claim are deterrents to war. What is really going on?

a)   Are the Soviet and American leaderships really considering starting a nuclear war which they can hope to win?

b)   Are they trying to destroy each other's economies through massive armament spendings and so breed unrest and instability?

c)   Are the Military – Industrial – Scientific Complexes (MISC) of America and Russia pushing along the arms race to keep themselves in jobs?

d)   Are both leaderships either mad or stupid?

Whatever the answer or answers, there is one evident factor; their policies are leading to the risk of all-out nuclear war which, as we have seen, would mean the end of our world.

The Problems of Winning a Nuclear War

Anyone considering launching a first-strike against an enemy must be certain to overcome the following problems.

1.   Missiles are accurate, but is their accuracy sufficient to wipe out the enemy's forces? Such is the power of nuclear weapons that only a small proportion are needed for a devastating retaliation. A first-strike requires *absolute certainty of success.* Something which does not exist.

2.   Even when a first-strike is launched an enemy would still have time to retaliate because the enemy could launch missiles as soon as the other side's showed up on radar screens. However, the use of the electro-magnetic pulse (EMP) effect of nuclear explosions, could destroy an enemy's ability to know when an attack was coming.

3.   Any first-strike would still leave submarine launched ballistic missiles (SLBMs) untouched and able to release destruction against an enemy.

In a normal, sane and well-balanced world you can only conclude that any idea of a winnable nuclear war is nonsense, but is the world a normal, sane and well-balanced place?

Conventional versus Nuclear War

We know that if a war started in Europe the use of nuclear weapons would be almost immediate. NATO does have a policy of using nuclear weapons *first* to stop the advance of Russian tank armies. Most people agree that once nuclear weapons are used the struggle will grow into all-out nuclear war.

Various plans have been put forward to avoid the use of nuclear weapons in any war by substituting conventional or non-nuclear weapons.

The case for conventional weapons runs as follows:

1.   The Western Alliance can field armies which would outnumber the Russians by two to one. We have

more people than they do; we could therefore expect through sheer weight of numbers to stop them if they ever attacked.

2. Such is the complexity and lethality of present-day conventional weapons that we could expect to destroy Russian armies without a lengthy struggle.

3. The fire-power of conventional weapons means that relatively few troops are required to use them and so we could avoid the unpopular idea of conscripting thousands of young people into the armed services.

4. Finally, and most important of all, the removal of the threat to use nuclear weapons early on in a battle could mean that a conflict would never escalate into all-out nuclear war.

The case against conventional weapons runs as follows:

1. Any action which signalled to an enemy that they could not expect to be faced with immediate and first-use of nuclear weapons might be taken as a sign of weakness. A sign that you would never use nuclear weapons at any level. This might tempt an enemy to start a war.

2. If nuclear weapons were not used almost immediately in a war by either side and a conventional struggle took place; what would happen if one side started to lose that war? Might they not be pushed into using nuclear weapons anyway to stop your advance?

TASKS: Chapter 16

1. It has been said that without nuclear deterrence World War III would have been fought by now. Find reasons for and against this statement.

2. Look at the points given on pages 77–8 that seek to explain the most recent advances in nuclear weaponry. Are any of them a likely explanation? Explain.

17 Britain and the bomb

Why Britain Got the Bomb

The first British atomic bomb was successfully exploded on Monte Bello island off the coast of Australia in 1952.

At that time Britain could still claim to be a great power; which means a country that has considerable influence in the world. There were only two other countries that could claim to be great powers — the United States and the Soviet Union. Possession of the bomb was like a badge which showed you were a member of the 'great power club'. As Britain considered itself to be a great power it was natural to acquire one of the marks of a great power; in this case, the bomb.

Britain, as today, was an ally of the United States. The Americans had enough bombs to protect Britain and Europe from the threat of a Soviet attack; Britain did not need the bomb for its own protection. However, there is, in this country, a strong tradition of self-reliance; a desire to control our own fate; to depend on no one but ourselves. This tradition is a deep one and in our history we have survived attacks and won victories when we have stood alone against an enemy. This tradition goes on to say that Britain is somehow stronger when it stands alone. For a country with this sort of background to get nuclear weapons seemed an obvious thing to do; for a nation that might one day have to stand alone again it was an essential requirement. Britain with the bomb would be at no one's mercy; most of all the Russians, and dependent on nobody; most of all the Americans.

It was thought that Britain with the bomb would be treated as an equal with the Americans and Russians. When events of world importance had to be decided then we would be listened to and take part in these decisions.

Financially the bomb was cheaper than a large conventional army, navy and air force; which meant that the bomb could kill more people more cheaply than any other sort of weapon.

All British governments since 1945 have had a sneaking suspicion that the American promise to defend Europe from attack might not be kept. As we have seen, this promise involves the use of nuclear weapons in a war in such a way that the United States itself might be destroyed. The nagging worry that the Americans would not really commit suicide for the sake of Europe led us to acquire the bomb so that if the Americans deserted us we, standing alone, would be able to deter a Russian attack on Britain.

So Britain acquired the bomb for the following reasons:

a) to maintain its position as a great power;

b) a desire for self-reliance;

c) to be treated as equally as important as the United States and the Soviet Union;

d) financially, nuclear weapons are the cheapest method of waging war; and

e) to deter a Russian attack if the Americans failed to defend us.

HMS Revenge

Why Britain Keeps the Bomb

Over thirty years have gone by since Britain acquired nuclear weapons. Do the reasons for their acquisition still hold true today?

The idea that the bomb would stamp us as a great power and give us a seat at the table with the Americans and Russians as an equal has sunk without trace. The events of the past thirty years have confirmed that Britain is no longer a power of world importance and we are not listened to as equals by the United States or the Soviet Union. In reality our closest ally, America, very often makes moves which could affect us directly and tells us about them afterwards.

The financial reason is still valid; nuclear weapons remain the least expensive form of mass extermination.

Two of the original reasons for getting the bomb still hold good; the standing alone idea and the deterrence idea. In addition to these original reasons two others have emerged to justify our retention of nuclear weapons.

One is the so-called 'second centre of decision' idea, which says that decisions for the Russians on the use of nuclear weapons would be a lot easier, a great deal more simple, if they only had to think about the intentions of one enemy — the United States. We complicate matters for them; we might confuse them, make them think twice about any thought of attack on the West. They must wonder whether in the case of a nuclear war our weapons are really controlled by us alone or by NATO.

The other new reason is that France has got nuclear weapons. France was the traditional enemy of Britain; we have fought more wars against the French than anyone else. Britain has always feared French domination of Europe. Despite having fought alongside the French in two world wars against Germany the tradition of dislike and fear has lingered on particularly among certain politicians and the military. After 1945 Britain soon realised that it was no longer a 'big fish in a big pond', but it could be a 'big fish in a little pond' below the level of the Americans and Russians but above the level of the French.

The major area of debate surrounding Britain's possession of nuclear weapons does not centre on either of these new reasons but on one of the original ones — deterrence. Remember that deterrence means preventing an enemy attack through certain knowledge that you will reply to an attack and cause your enemy unacceptable damage.

The first question to ask is: Would Britain's nuclear weapons *by themselves* deter a Russian attack on this country?

British weapons are meant to deter an attack by threatening the destruction of Moscow, the Soviet capital; although other cities could be added because we have sufficient power to destroy many more. The important point, however, is that the damage we could inflict on the Russians is *partial*; we could not destroy all their population centres. On the other hand the damage they could inflict on us could be *total*; they could lay waste all of our towns and cities and make the rest of the country uninhabitable.

The second question, therefore, is: would any British Prime Minister, knowing that we could be totally destroyed after inflicting only partial damage on the Soviet Union ever order our weapons to be used?

This is the most serious decision any Prime Minister could ever be called upon to make. This question, however, is not ours alone to answer. The effectiveness or credibility of the British deterrent depends to a large extent on what the Russian leadership believes we would do.

Does the Russian leadership believe we would ever use our nuclear weapons knowing that by doing so we are inviting total destruction? The Russians would have to decide whether or not our deterrent threat is just a bluff or deadly serious.

In the words of Field Marshal Lord Carver,

I can conceive of no circumstances in which it would be right, responsible or realistic for the Prime Minister of the United Kingdom to authorise the use of British nuclear weapons . . . nor do I believe that the Russians would believe it to be a realistic assumption that he or she would.
(*The Times,* May 1980.)

There are perhaps two circumstances in which it is imaginable that Britain might use its nuclear weapons against the Soviet Union:

a)   madness on the part of a Prime Minister; and

b)   if a Prime Minister faced with the prospect of a Russian occupation of this country decided we would all be better off *dead than red*.

Better Dead than Red. When this phrase is used it usually is taken to mean that the worst aspects of the Soviet regime would be forced upon the British people — a police State, no political opposition, no free speech, forced labour and prison camps. That life in this country would be so changed, so completely intolerable that death might be the easiest solution to the problem. Those who disagree with this idea have the opposite slogan.

Better Red than Dead. This claims that a Russian or 'red' occupation of this country might be a dreadful thing for us at first, but as time went by things would improve. The Russians would find such difficulty in suppressing a nation of 55 million that they would eventually have to make life easier for us. The people who support this argument would say that anything is better than the destruction of the British people; for where there is life, there is hope.

Unilateral versus Multilateral Disarmament

The existence of doubt about the *certain* use of British nuclear weapons has led some people in this country to ask why we keep them at all. An argument has been going on for many years over what should be done about our nuclear weapons. This has come to be known as the unilateral versus multilateral disarmament debate.

Unilateral nuclear disarmament, which was mentioned earlier, means one-sided disarmament. You give up your armaments in the hope that others will follow your example and disarm as well.

There are three main kinds of unilateral nuclear disarmament.

a)   *Permanent;* which means all nuclear weapons are given up together with all the facilities needed to make them; you intend never to have them again.

b)   *Temporary;* where you are seen to get rid of your nuclear weapons but *not* the facilities needed to make them so that if no one follows your example by disarming themselves you can make the weapons again and return to your previous position.

ever its pitfalls it does offer a serious alternative in the disarmament issue.

Britain: Its Nuclear Timetable

1946 Work started on jet aircraft to carry 'special bomb'.

1947 Labour Government give the go-ahead for the construction of Britain's atomic bomb.

1952 Atom bomb successfully exploded at Monte Bello.

1956 British long-range V-bomber force becomes able to strike at the Soviet Union.

1957 Hydrogen bomb successfully exploded at Bikini Atoll in the Pacific Ocean.

1962 British Conservative Government negotiates a deal to buy American Polaris SLBMs to replace V-bomber force.

1969 Polaris SLBMs become main part of Britain's nuclear forces.

1978 Labour Government sets up working parties to consider a replacement for Polaris.

1979 Conservative Government negotiates a deal to buy the American Trident SLBM to replace Polaris by early 1990s.

1980 Conservative Government publicly announces Trident deal at a provisional cost of £4500 to £5000 million. By June 1985 the cost of Trident was put at £12 000 million.

c) *Nuclear to conventional deterrence;* here nuclear weapons are given up permanently but money is spent on conventional defence.

Multilateral disarmament means many-sided disarmament whereby all nuclear States agree to disarm by gradual phases so that each country can feel secure from attack.

Of the two, multilateral disarmament sounds more sensible, more acceptable than unilateral disarmament, but remembering the lack of progress in multilateral nuclear disarmament you can understand why the unilateralist case has become a matter of public interest and debate. What-

Britain: Its Nuclear Armoury

The British Army has two kinds of nuclear weaponry:

a) *short-range Lance* missiles, 1 warhead each, for use in a war in

Europe — numbers 60 to possibly 264; and

b) *nuclear artillery* — sixteen 8″ howitzers, fifty 155 mm howitzers, and FH-70 howitzers (new, numbers unknown). Weaponry for use in land battles in Europe as a part of NATO's flexible response policy.

M 109 155mm Self-propelled Howitzer

The Royal Air Force has:

a) 60 Buccaneers carrying 2 nuclear weapons each;
b) 72 Jaguars, carrying 1 nuclear weapon each; and
c) 28 Nimrods carrying 2 nuclear depth charges each for use against enemy submarines.

The Royal Air Force will replace 36 Buccaneers with 220 Tornado strike aircraft each carrying 2 nuclear weapons. The Tornado is an all-weather, low level attack plane intended to avoid Soviet radar systems; the Tornado represents a significant increase in Britain's nuclear strike capability. The first Tornado squadron came into active service during 1984.

The Royal Navy has:

a) 64 Polaris SLBMs;
b) 60 Sea King/Wasp/Wessex/Lynx helicopters each carrying nuclear depth charges; and
c) 24 Sea Harriers capable of attacks on submarines or land-based targets, assumed to carry 1 nuclear weapon each.

The Royal Navy will have 512 Trident D5 warheads to replace the 64 Polaris warheads by the early 1990s. Trident D5 will represent an enormous increase in Britain's nuclear strike power. Trident like most recent missiles is highly accurate.

Although most debate in this country centres around the cost and power

Tornado aircraft

represented by Trident the list above does show that Britain has many more nuclear weapons for use in many varieties of conflict.
(Source: *The Military Balance: International Institute for Strategic Studies,* London 1982.)

All British nuclear weapons are committed to NATO forces in Western Europe under the control of an American serviceman. Britain, however, reserves the right to control and use these weapons whenever national interests are at stake.

centres in Russia than it can with Polaris. The damage we could inflict on the Russians will be a lot higher.

What effects will this have? Will it mean the disappearance of any lingering doubt the Russians may have had about the seriousness of our threat to use our deterrent? Or, because Trident is a highly accurate first-strike weapon, will the Russians see it merely as an addition to NATO's already formidable nuclear arsenal?

Trident and Deterrence

By the early 1990s, when Trident is fully operational, the British armed forces will be able to target many more population

Comment This diagram shows the different nuclear deterrents open to a British Government. The Government has chosen Trident D5, the most expensive option, presumably because they believe it to be the most effective.

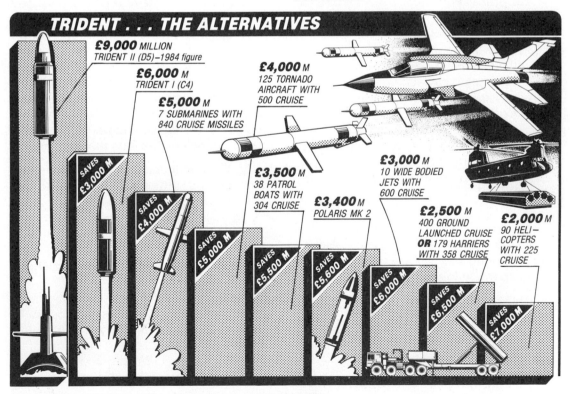

TRIDENT . . . THE ALTERNATIVES

£9,000 MILLION
TRIDENT II (D5)–1984 figure

£6,000 M
TRIDENT I (C4)

£5,000 M
7 SUBMARINES WITH 840 CRUISE MISSILES

£4,000 M
125 TORNADO AIRCRAFT WITH 500 CRUISE

£3,500 M
38 PATROL BOATS WITH 304 CRUISE

£3,400 M
POLARIS MK 2

£3,000 M
10 WIDE BODIED JETS WITH 600 CRUISE

£2,500 M
400 GROUND LAUNCHED CRUISE **OR** 179 HARRIERS WITH 358 CRUISE

£2,000 M
90 HELI-COPTERS WITH 225 CRUISE

SAVES £3,000 M
SAVES £4,000 M
SAVES £5,000 M
SAVES £5,500 M
SAVES £5,600 M
SAVES £6,000 M
SAVES £6,500 M
SAVES £7,000 M

Note By June 1985 cost of Trident D5 had risen to £12,000 million

18 Scenario for the future

At 3 o'clock on the afternoon of 18 March the Prime MInister rose to address the House of Commons; his statement was short and to the point.

After due consideration and consultation Her Majesty's Government has decided to take the following courses of action.

1. An immediate freeze on the production, testing and deployment of all British nuclear weapons.
2. The cancellation of nuclear weapons at present on order from the United States.
3. A gradual and phased run-down of existing British nuclear weapons and all facilities for their manufacture.
4. A complete closedown of the civilian nuclear power programme, existing or planned.
5. The setting-up of a working party to produce a blueprint for a non-nuclear or conventional defence system for the United Kingdom.

The Prime Minister then went on to say:

This decision, one of the most far-reaching ever made by a British government, has been taken in order to achieve the following objectives.

1. By our example to bring about complete nuclear disarmament in the world; other countries will follow the road which we have now opened up for them.
2. To make it plain to the Soviet Union that we will no longer pose a nuclear threat to them and therefore we should no longer be regarded as a target for nuclear attack.

I will be sending the following letter to the Soviet leader, Mr Zinoviev, the US President, Jerry Baines; copies will also be despatched to the governments of France and China.

The Prime Minister opened the letter and after a brief, nervous cough he read it out.

The decision we have taken marks a new step forward; it is the first and most necessary move to bring an end to the madness of the nuclear arms race which threatens to engulf and destroy every man, woman and child on earth.

It is Her Majesty's Government's most earnest hope that you will give our decision serious consideration and come to the same conclusions that we have.

As the Prime Minister sat down a deathly hush descended upon the normally noisy House of Commons. The silence did not last very long as the impact of his statement sank in very quickly. The Prime Minister braced himself for the flood of questions and probably abuse which was bound to fall on him.

The Speaker of the House of Commons sat motionless and expressionless as he looked at the forest of arms raised around him. He noticed Sid Clapper, the Member for Forest East, who red-faced and jabbing an angry finger at the Prime Minister shouted:

The Prime Minister has just announced

measures which, in effect, amount to a declaration of unilateral nuclear disarmament; yet not once did he use those words because if he had then the nation would be instantly outraged. Unilateral disarmament leaves us defenceless. The Prime Minister has sold us down the river; he is not a true Englishman; he's lower than the lowest traitor.

The Speaker called upon the Prime Minister who was already on his feet waiting to reply.

I am just as much a patriot as the Hon. Member. Until recently Britain has usually been at the forefront of world events; what better way for us to lead the world again as the first country to give up weapons of mass extermination.

We are not going to be defenceless. You heard me announce plans for a detailed non-nuclear defence. This will involve a huge boost for our armed services.

The questions came fast and furious as the afternoon drew on. The Prime Minister had been briefed on what to expect and he handled most of the questions in a calm and competent manner: 'Why has the Prime Minister decided to close down our civilian nuclear power programme? We need this as an alternative source of energy to coal, gas and oil.'

The Prime Minister answered:

Even when we no longer have a single nuclear weapon we will still be a target for attack because from nuclear power we can gain the materials needed to make nuclear weapons. No one is going to believe in our sincerity as long as we still have the means to make these weapons. We must be seen to genuinely give up all means of making nuclear weapons.

The attacks continued.

The Prime Minister, in a short speech, has just degraded our whole nation before the world. What he has done is to make obvious his desire to take Britain out of the frontline; to shoulder less responsibility for the burden of dealing with the world's problems. The political impact will be disastrous among both our enemies and our friends. Certainly as long as France retains nuclear weapons it will show a renouncing of power and influence.

The Prime Minister believes that unilateral disarmament will make the Russians remove us from their list of nuclear targets. I don't believe that will happen. The Russians will take what has happened here today as an act of weakness. We will be a target in a war with or without our deterrent. We are too important to be left alone. Everyone here knows what happens when you show a sign of weakness to a bully — you get a kick in the face. The Russians will blackmail us.

The Prime Minister was once more on his feet:

Mr Speaker, in reply to the previous statements I say that anyone who thinks we ought to keep our nuclear weapons because the French have got them is living in a different century. People like that ought to glance at the calendar when they get up in the morning — this is the twentieth century not any other. And anyway I have called upon the French to disarm along with us; I am sure that they will look at what we have done in the best possible light.

As to the idea that we will be blackmailed or still be a nuclear target after nuclear disarmament I must disagree. I see the intentions of the Russians differently. I believe what we are doing will shake up the world and lead to multilateral nuclear disarmament.

More questions followed, some hostile,

some friendly, some merely seeking clarification or further information.

It was just after 6 o'clock that a tired, but quietly satisfied Prime Minister rose to make his final statement to the House. He remembered what should have been the final sentence of that statement '. . . I could never imagine giving the order for a nuclear attack on the Soviet Union knowing full well that I would be signing the death warrant of the British people.'

He sank down on his seat; loosened his tie and was only vaguely aware of the rain of abuse from the Opposition benches; the words came at him: 'Coward — Traitor — How much are the Russians paying you? — Shoulder your responsibilities — You have left us defenceless.'

He got up and walked slowly and calmly away from the noise, but he could not resist getting in the last word so he turned and faced the angry people, raised his arm at them and shouted,

> You all know full well that the Russians won't harm us, they are too frightened of what the Americans will do to them.

It was a silly thing to say. The words rang in his head as he left the House of Commons and made his way to his car. It was dark, but he thought the clocks will go forward an hour next week; an hour's extra light; perhaps it was a sign of hope for him. As he neared his car a figure came alongside him; it was his political adviser and closest friend. And in a quiet voice he said, 'At least they didn't get round to asking you about the American bases — but they will.'

A Visit from 'the Human Iceberg'

During all the discussions leading up to the decision to disarm, the issue of the American bases in Britain, the question of American cruise missiles at Greenham and

Molesworth, and membership of NATO had cropped up.

A few days after his election victory the Prime Minister had a meeting with the Chief of the Defence Staff during which he learned for the first time the full details of American involvement in Britain. He had spent a few hours before the meeting thumbing through all the documents left for him the day before by a member of the Defence Staff. He glanced down at the map showing American bases in Britain. He had seen it before, in 1980, when it had been published.

His mind wandered away from the map; there seemed so much to do, so many obstacles to overcome if he was to achieve his aim of a Britain without nuclear weapons; a Britain safe from nuclear destruction. His train of thought was interrupted by a sharp knock on his office door. He looked up straight into the pale blue eyes of Field Marshal Sir James Doubleday, Chief of the Defence Staff — nickname 'the human iceberg'.

'You have read the stuff about our membership of NATO, Prime Minister.'

The Prime Minister opened his mouth to reply, but the Field Marshal went straight on, 'Then you agree with our membership.'

'Yes, but . . .'

'Yes, but what, Prime Minister?'

The Prime Minister felt annoyance rising within him; for someone with the reputation of being cold and calculating, the 'human iceberg' could certainly arouse anger. The Prime Minister quickly suppressed his annoyance and calmly said, 'I am concerned, Field Marshal, about NATO's military policy; most of all its threat of "first-use" of nuclear weapons in a European war. Is it not possible to rely on conventional weapons to stop the Russians?'

'Of course it's possible, Prime Minister, but you know the thought of nuclear weapons waiting for them certainly stops the Russians even considering an attack,

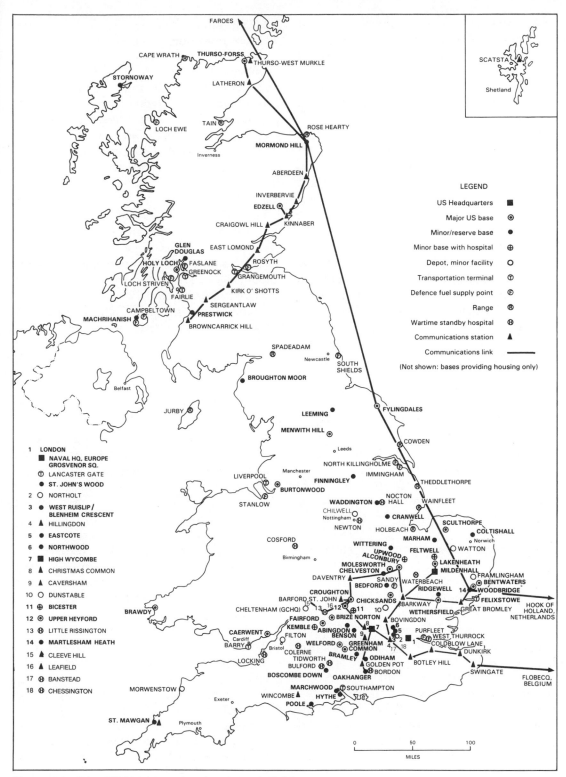

The map the Prime Minister saw – American bases in Britain

and in addition, Prime Minister, might I say that conventional defence could mean a return to conscription in this country. I don't think that you politicians would like the unpopularity that would bring; eighteen-year-olds taken away from home and into the Services.'

Leaning over the Prime Minister's desk, the Field Marshal whispered, 'Just got the chance to vote then, haven't they?'

Both men stared at each other; a thought flashed through the Prime Minister's mind, 'This man is threatening me.'

The Field Marshal dropped his gaze and in a matter of fact voice began the lecture which he had carefully prepared. He knew that the man in front of him had been elected on a platform that committed Britain to get rid of its nuclear weapons. The Field Marshal's main concern was to make sure that the new Prime Minister did not pursue any half-baked or mad schemes about withdrawal from NATO or removing American bases.

'NATO, Prime Minister, is the cornerstone of Britain's security. NATO, because it has nuclear weapons and threatens to use them first in a conflict with the Russians, has kept the peace in Europe for many years.'

Although he'd heard all the arguments before the Prime Minister was compelled by the force of the Field Marshal's words to remain attentive.

'You know why we wanted NATO to come about?'

'Yes, I believe so.'

'Then you will know, Prime Minister, that it's meant to keep the Germans down, the Russians out and the Americans in. If we do not play a full part in it the Western Alliance will crumble.'

The Prime Minister knew that after World War II the conquerors of Germany — America, Britain and Russia — had disagreed on many issues, but they did agree that Germany should never again be in a position to militarily dominate Europe.

NATO had been one way to achieve this by involving the new West German State in a complex military alliance controlled by an American serviceman. The Russians had done the same to the eastern part of Germany by including it in the Warsaw Pact.

The Field Marshal now turned his attention to the Americans and Russians.

'We need the Americans; without them you know full well what would happen, the Russians would dominate Western Europe. Mark my words, Prime Minister, the Soviet Union is intent on world revolution; if it controlled Western Europe it would have the means to achieve this.

'The map of American bases you were looking at when I came in; that is how we involve the Americans here.'

'It may involve them, Field Marshal, but do we have any control over the bases?'

'Er — no, Prime Minister.'

'Do we know what goes on in them?'

'The Americans tell us a great deal about their activities.'

'You mean, Field Marshal, they tell us what they want us to know.'

'You could put it that way, Prime Minister.'

There was a pause as the Prime Minister read through another document on his desk.

'Cruise missiles, Field Marshal, what about them? They are American; do we have any control over their use?'

'Of course we do.'

'What precisely does that mean?' the Prime Minister responded sharply.

'It means, Prime Minister, that you would be consulted by the Americans and a joint decision arrived at before they could be used.'

'Suppose, Field Marshal, time was very limited; suppose there was a crisis — what then?'

'The agreement would still hold good, Prime Minister.'

'Really, Field Marshal?' The Prime Minister's disbelief was obvious.

'Tell me, Field Marshal, do we have any

real control over them; can we stop them being fired by the Americans?'

'No, Prime Minister, we can't; except of course by using our troops to take over the missile bases.' The Field Marshal gave half a smile as he said this, as if the whole idea was amusing.

'Thank you, Field Marshal, I think that concludes our meeting.'

The Chief of the Defence Staff rose, shook the Prime Minister's hand and turned for the door; as he opened the door he looked back at the Prime Minister and said very firmly, 'Prime Minister, the details about bases and cruise missiles are not important. What is important is that the British Government makes every effort to keep the Americans committed to and involved with the defence of this country. If war does come it is vital that American servicemen in Europe get killed; the more the better, Prime Minister. The Americans get very emotional when their men are killed; a few thousand dead Americans would certainly make sure the United States got involved in the conflict.'

'The Field Marshal and I are not going to be friends,' thought the Prime Minister, but at least the man seemed straight and honest in his views. The Prime Minister stared out of the window and his mind went over the conversation with the Field Marshal. 'Details not important; of course they are important,' he blurted out aloud. He reached for his telephone, spoke into it and a few minutes later the documents he had asked for were on his desk. He flicked through the pages of the old newspaper clippings, most of them from the late 1970s and early 1980s; they were all to do with the deployment of American cruise missiles in Britain. He remembered the events as if they were yesterday. The pictures of the women at Greenham Common sitting round their camp fires. There was even a picture of himself when he had made a visit to Greenham to hand out money for the 'cause'.

The articles covered the Russian response to the deployment of Cruise; the warnings were quite clear:

Cruise missiles are a part of the American plan to start a nuclear war.

Any country which receives cruise missiles will be a nuclear target.

And then the American views:

Cruise missiles will strengthen the West's deterrent capability.

Cruise missiles are not part of any plan to start a nuclear war.

The Prime Minister looked through page after page of clippings until he found those he really wanted; his eyes settled on one in particular which directly contradicted the views given by the Field Marshal, it read:

The decision to use nuclear weapons in Europe is purely a US decision. One of the great myths that's been perpetrated in Europe is that somehow the [European] NATO countries will have something to say about whether or not the US uses nuclear weapons. They will not. Washington may consult with its European allies . . . and may take their advice or may not, but if the US decides to use nuclear weapons there's nobody in Europe that could stop us.
(This is taken from an actual quote by Admiral Gene La Rocque, Director of the Centre for Defense Information, Washington DC, in the *Guardian,* 24/2/ 83.)

The Prime Minister read the article over and over again. He had always known that to make the country safe from a nuclear attack unilateral nuclear disarmament was not enough. The presence of American bases with their bombers, fighters and cruise missiles still made Britain an obvious candidate for nuclear destruction and although his speech to the House of

Commons was to deliberately avoid mention of these issues he knew one thing for certain — the Americans would have to go.

The Day after the Prime Minister's Speech

The morning after his speech he overslept; his first recollection that a new day had dawned was a rough hand shaking his shoulder. Bleary-eyed, he stared up at his political adviser who thrust some paper into his hand. He rolled out of bed and, still only half awake, began to look at the notes. The first read:

FROM THE OFFICE OF THE PRESIDENT OF THE UNITED STATES OF AMERICA

The United States Government applauds the decision taken by Her Majesty's Government. The United States will do all in its power to pursue the initiative set by Her Majesty's Government.

The Prime Minister knew the Americans would not object to his move over unilateral disarmament. They had never liked Britain's independent deterrent. They saw it as a nuisance, an unnecessary complication to their own nuclear plans.

The second note was headed:

FROM THE FIRST SECRETARY OF THE CENTRAL COMMITTEE OF THE COMMUNIST PARTY OF THE SOVIET UNION

The people of the Soviet Union salute the decision of the British Government as a landmark of peace and progress.

He could not have expected any more than this; these were immediate and hasty reactions. Time alone would tell whether his government's decision would go down in history as the greatest peace initiative of all time or the act of political fools and incompetents.

After breakfast the Prime Minister chaired a full meeting of the Cabinet. He sat, only half-listening, as the Secretary to the Cabinet droned on about the details of Britain's nuclear run-down. At the end of the long table sat the chiefs of the armed services, there by special invitation. As the announcement was made that Trident D5 SLBMs were to be instantly withdrawn from service the Prime Minister saw a flicker of distaste and near-hatred cross the face of his navy chief. The last time he had seen the Admiral-of-the-Fleet that same face was wreathed in smiles. It was a few months ago when they had met to talk about the future of the Navy. The Prime Minister had not uttered one word about unilateral disarmament to the Admiral; something which he now felt slightly guilty about.

Talk about Trident

The details about Trident missiles which the Prime Minister had before him at the meeting with the Admiral were mostly well known, nonetheless he read them as the Admiral sat quietly waiting for him to finish.

The paper headed 'Trident D5 Missile System' was in the form of short notes which read:

Trident missile purchase agreement date with the United States: July 1980. Missile of US manufacture: warhead, British. Four nuclear submarines carry Trident; British built.

Polaris missiles and submarines could not guarantee deterrence credibility into the twenty-first century. Trident ensures we can penetrate Soviet defence systems and equally ensures against detection and destruction by Soviet hunter-killer submarines.

COMPARISON OF FIREPOWER — POLARIS AND TRIDENT

	WARHEADS PER MISSILE	TOTAL TARGETS	ACCURACY IN YARDS	RANGE IN MILES
POLARIS	3 MRV	64	985	2500
TRIDENT	8 MARV	512	33 approx.	7500

The Prime Minister finished reading and looked up at the Admiral. 'I can see easily that having 512 targets to hit rather than 64 and Trident's ability to launch an attack far away from enemy detection must have made it a more attractive proposition from your point of view, Admiral.'

The Prime Minister then picked up a pencil and ringed the column headed 'Accuracy in Yards'.

'We are supposed to deter the Russians, Admiral; if that failed we would have to destroy their population centres. We don't need accuracy down to the level of a few yards to do that; do we?'

'Of course we don't, Prime Minister.'

'Admiral, the Russians believe Trident is a first-strike weapon; a weapon that could be used to start and very hopefully win a nuclear war. Are they going to believe us when we claim it is a deterrent weapon to be used only *after* they have attacked us? How can we prove it is a deterrent weapon and not intended as a first-strike weapon?

The Admiral paused, he seemed a little ill-at-ease. 'With all due respect, Prime Minister, that's not my problem; that's something for the politicians to sort out. All I know is that Trident is the best available weapon for the Royal Navy. We can't make our own missiles, we have to accept what the Americans have on offer and they only make missiles with a high accuracy rating.'

The Prime Minister knew the Admiral was right. He believed the Admiral saw Trident purely as a deterrent weapon; it was the job of the politicians; his job to convince the people in Moscow that it was a deterrent weapon. But how was he to do that? Suddenly he stopped short in his train of thought. It would not be a problem because Trident would soon be scrapped!

The Admiral stared down the long table at the Prime Minister; he did not like him; he must have known at that meeting about the fate of Trident, he thought, and yet he gave no indication whatsoever. The pride and joy of the Navy; the British nuclear deterrent, condemned to the scrap-heap. The Admiral tried to suppress his feelings of annoyance with the Prime Minister, but they would not go away.

The meeting dragged on long past the Prime Minister's usual lunch hour; he was hungry and still a little tired; he adjourned the meeting.

He had lunch with his Minister of Defence; a young ambitious man; young enough to take the strain that the weeks ahead promised to bring. It was his job to deal with the details of nuclear disarmament; a task which meant close co-operation with the chiefs of the Army, Navy and Airforce. The Prime Minister did not envy the young man that job!

He leaned across the table to his minister, who was just raising his first spoonful of soup to his lips, and said jokingly, 'Are the military going to shoot us for what we have done? Safe in our beds are we?'

The spoon fell from the Defence

supporters Uncles Geoff and Ernest, but only Uncle Cyril spoke, the rest just nodded with agreement at everything he said.

'As a family we've had our ups and downs, our quarrels; but by and large we have done pretty well for ourselves. We don't go short of food and we have a decent house to live in. You want to know why? He did not wait for an answer but went on.

'Because we in the H of H group have seen to it that no other family has taken away what we own. We've got a bread shop, a greengrocery, a petrol station, and a DIY shop. Over the years we have built up a safe and prosperous living for the family.

'You know the sort of neighbourhood this is; the police are frightened to walk the streets; it's a rough place, but we can walk the streets because we are bigger and stronger than anyone else and we've got to keep it that way.

'We've had to fight in the past to keep the peace around here and I'm very sorry to say it looks now that we are going to have to fight again. The family that lives at the red and white house down the road are starting to get above themselves. Why only yesterday they threatened a friend of ours; they've been hanging around our petrol station looking menacing and they have been saying nasty things about us in the neighbourhood.

'I know what this means. I've seen it all before as a young man. Take it from me these people are dangerous. They are after everything we have and if they get it you are *all* out in the cold. We need to be strong to fight them. But above all we must stick together as a family; we need unity; no more quarrels. We must make every effort to stop them or they will stop us; all of us!'

Uncle Cyril sat down. Plan C did work; the troublemakers either behaved or nobody took any notice of them any more. Uncle Cyril's speech and the fear of the family in the red and white house had done the trick.

The same day Uncle Ernest took you and

some of the others down to the DIY shop; you spent the day making bigger and better clubs than those that the family in the red and white house had.

> In order to make the country bear the burden, we have to create an emotional atmosphere akin to war-time psychology. We have to create the idea of a threat from without.
> (John Foster Dulles, former US Secretary of State.)

This version of the Cold War claims that the people who rule both America and Russia and those who gain most from those systems want to see them continue. It says that the real point of the Cold War is to keep ruling groups in their positions of relative power and wealth.

One of the oldest ways that ruling groups have kept themselves in power is to use fear of an outside enemy as a way to unite their people; put down troublemakers and make everyone pull together.

In fact this version of the Cold War goes even further than this and states that the real enemy of the United States is not the Soviet Union at all, but Western Europe and Japan.

The reasons given for this are as follows: After World War II Europe and Japan were bankrupt, defeated and destroyed; literally down and out. The United States came out of the war untouched and economically strong. In its search for future prosperity and therefore political stability the United States took over European and Japanese export markets in Latin America, the Middle and Far East and has remained determined to keep them. The Soviet Union, with its inefficient economic system, has never been and does not look like being an economic threat to the United States.

As Europe and Japan revived economically during the 1950s the United States attempted to make European countries pay more and more money into armaments production using fear of the Soviet Union to do this. Money spent on re-arming could not be used overseas to

Minister's hand, landed in the middle of his soup and splashed the dark brown fluid all over the tablecloth. He looked up at the Prime Minister and said, 'I don't know.'

He was definitely *not* joking.

Facing the Media

The news of Britain's decision to disarm unilaterally had spread quickly. Political leaders in the capitals of the world assessed how the decision would affect them and their countries.

The door of the Prime Minister's home at 10 Downing Street was besieged by reporters. Television cameras were there; an anxious reporter looked at the camera that was beamed on him.

'There's no sign of him yet. He's expected back from lunch soon. We hope to have more news for you then. This is Jeff Jones for "News at 2.30" on the steps of 10 Downing Street, returning you to the studio.'

The Prime Minister finished his lunch thinking about his colleague's remark. The idea that the military might cause trouble had only fleetingly crossed his mind. They had a long tradition of obedience to their political masters. His proposal for a non-nuclear defence system would give them more men and more money. They never had liked the idea of a war fought with nuclear weapons. They would have loved to go back to the old days when they would show off their brilliance as commanders and leaders of men. Nuclear war could be fought by people in white coats who pressed buttons. The idea of trouble from the military seemed nonsense.

The Prime Minister's schedule that afternoon included a recording for television about defence policy. It had been arranged weeks before and he saw no reason to cancel it; after all it was a golden opportunity to explain to the nation the full con-sequences of his speech to the House of Commons the day before.

He arrived at the studio, was welcomed by the television people and after a brief visit to the make-up room was ushered into a small room to watch the first part of the programme. He sat and watched the small monitor screen as the programme presenter introduced the feature.

Good evening and welcome to this week's edition of 'Britain in Action'; as most of you will know the Prime Minister astounded the world yesterday afternoon by announcing that Britain will no longer be a nuclear State; all our nuclear weapons are going on the scrap-heap. We have the Prime Minister with us this evening and we will be talking to him later on, but first let's take a look at Britain without nuclear weapons; how would we defend ourselves? Is defence possible at all?

A caption came onto the screen that read,

BRITAIN'S NON-NUCLEAR or
ALTERNATIVE DEFENCE
FACT or FANTASY

The programme presenter went on.

A lot of work went on in the early 1980s directed at the problem of defending Britain and Western Europe against attack without using nuclear weapons. As far as our membership of the Western alliance system, NATO, is concerned the main suggestions put forward were these:

(Again, captions came on to the screen.)

BRITAIN SHOULD WITHDRAW FROM
NATO UNLESS NATO DID THE
FOLLOWING THINGS:

1. AGREED NOT TO USE NUCLEAR
   WEAPONS *FIRST* IN ANY WAR
2. AGREED TO WITHDRAW SHORT-

RANGE BATTLEFIELD NUCLEAR
WEAPONS
3. AGREED TO WITHDRAW *ALL* NUCLEAR
   WEAPONS TARGETED ON EUROPE
4. EUROPE SHOULD TELL THE UNITED
   STATES TO WITHDRAW ITS THREAT TO
   USE NUCLEAR WEAPONS AGAINST
   RUSSIA IF THE RUSSIANS ATTACKED
   EUROPE.

The presenter continued.

The ideas of alternative defence, having
dealt with NATO and nuclear weaponry,
then go on to talk about the actual
defence of Europe and Britain using
conventional weapons only. The major
point here is that we should have no
offensive weapons, but be able to inflict
heavy and unacceptable losses on an
invader. This is called 'in depth territorial
defence' and such a defence is based on
the 'porcupine principle' which means we
become hard for an enemy to swallow

and even harder to digest. This is what
the battle line in Europe could look like:

(A diagram came on the screen showing
the possible battlefield formations using
conventional weaponry only.)

The Prime Minister watched the screen
carefully; the diagram looked impressive; a
young lady put her head round the door of
his room and asked him if he wanted a cup
of coffee. He said that he did. As he turned
back to the screen he saw the programme
presenter talking to General Sir Ian
Farthing; now retired from active service,
but still very active on the nation's television
screens.
'So you believe that such a defence
system could stop the Russians, General.'
'If what we have seen is actually the sort of
defence we would set up then I would say
that it stands a good chance of stopping tank
armies.'

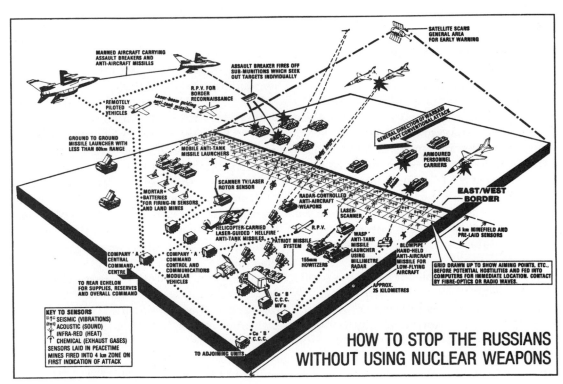

HOW TO STOP THE RUSSIANS
WITHOUT USING NUCLEAR WEAPONS

'So because of this alternative defence system we are not defenceless if we get rid of nuclear weapons.'

'Well', Sir Ian paused slightly, 'yes and no.'

'What precisely does that mean, Sir Ian?'

'It means *yes* we can stop the Russians if they come at us with conventional weapons and *no* if they come at us with nuclear weapons.'

'So what you are saying, and correct me if I get it wrong, is that alternative defence depends for its success on the Russians playing the game according to our rules; being good boys and not using nuclear weapons.'

'Yes, that is precisely what I mean,' replied Sir Ian.

The Prime Minister had just finished his coffee when he was asked to come down to the studio. He took his seat in front of the cameras and the programme presenter went through the sorts of questions he was going to ask. The Prime Minister nodded his agreement with them.

'Prime Minister, thank you for giving up your valuable time to talk with us this evening; can I ask you first about your attitude to our membership of NATO. Do you agree that we should withdraw unless NATO gives up its nuclear weapons?'

'That is a question which the Government is still considering, however, may I say that as members of NATO we will be pushing for it to adopt a non-nuclear defence policy because to effectively defend Britain we need the whole of Western Europe to adopt the same defence posture that we will be setting up.'

'Have you a time scale for NATO to do this, Prime Minister?'

'As I said the Government is still considering what is after all a very complex issue; we have lots of people to consult before we can make a decision in the best interests of the British people.'

'If NATO does not give up nuclear weapons, Prime Minister, will Britain withdraw?'

'We would have to consider that option because we would have a defence policy based on conventional weapons whereas NATO would have a policy based on nuclear weapons.'

'When you say NATO must do certain things don't you really mean the United States.'

'Yes, basically, the United States will have to agree with our moves.'

'Do you think they will?'

'That remains to be seen.'

'You made no mention in your speech yesterday about the American bases in this country — what about them?'

'They remain something about which we will be talking to the Americans.'

'Prime Minister, you may have read about the suggestion that unilateral disarmament is really a non-starter; it can have no impact on the major powers; it will not make them disarm. Nor will it remove this country from the Russian's nuclear target list; that instead of unilateral disarmament you should have struck a deal directly with the Russians; a two-sided or bilateral deal.'

The Prime Minister interrupted, 'I think you are referring to the idea that if we gave up nuclear weapons then the Russians would simply agree to remove their missiles targeted on this country.'

'Yes, Prime Minister, that is what I meant.'

'Well, you misunderstand the purpose behind our unilateral move. Of course we could try to deal directly with the Russians about our weapons, about American nuclear forces in this country, with the aim of making us safe from nuclear attack. This is not an option that can be ruled out. However, the whole idea of unilateral disarmament is bigger and broader than any narrow deal we could hope to strike with the Russians.

'It is meant to open a new era of history; it

is meant to achieve, through our example, comprehensive multilateral nuclear disarmament. It is a grand gesture not a narrow-minded defeatist way out of nuclear devastation. I hope the world will see it that way; I hope the British people will see it that way and most of all I hope the Americans and the Russians, the French and the Chinese will see it that way.

'We have done what we have done out of the best possible motives. Britain has shown that there is a way out of the madness of the nuclear arms race. Generations as yet unborn will thank us for saving the world for them to live prosperous and decent lives.'

The Prime Minister's hand came down on the table with a measured thump. He thought that it was one of his better performances, perhaps a bit over the top, but still effective to the thousands sitting and watching at home. And he knew that he meant every word of it.

'Thank you, Prime Minister, that's all we have time for this evening: we now take you over direct to the Olympic stadium in Rome where a sensational last minute equaliser has kept England's chances of survival in this year's World Cup alive . . .'

The Prime Minister got up and walked slowly out of the studio. It was just over twenty-four hours since he rose to address the House of Commons.

The American Bases and NATO

He arrived back at 10 Downing Street; gave a few short interviews to the waiting reporters and quickly withdrew to his private office and picked up the day's newspapers.

The Press, not friendly to him, had given his decision a real roasting. As he flicked through the pages of one popular daily he stared at a particularly nasty cartoon which had used his last words to the House of Commons as its caption. It did not pull any punches. Most of the Press seemed determined to go after him and continue to go after him, but he knew he would not, could not reverse his decision.

UNILATERAL IS 'LOONYLATERAL'

NUCLEAR UMBRELLA HELD BY THE AMERICANS

UNCLE SAM U.S.A.

PRIME MINISTER OF BRITAIN

You all know... that the Russians won't harm us — they're too frightened of what the Americans will do to them!

He's worth his weight in roubles!

RUSSIAN BEAR

You're trusting someone else to hold the umbrella when it rains ??!!

THE COWARD'S 'PEACE' PLAN: WHAT FUTURE FOR A TOOTHLESS BRITAIN?

He spent the next two hours talking with his political adviser about NATO and the American bases. They were both trying to find some wording which would be acceptable to the rest of the Government. They both knew that the bases had to go; that Britain could not belong to an alliance which had the use of nuclear weapons as a prime element of its policy. The Prime Minister knew that this would be the most difficult stage of the operation to make Britain safe from nuclear attack.

The next morning the Cabinet meeting reconvened, without the service chiefs being there; there was very little argument over the necessity to act about American bases and NATO, but a good deal of discussion over the exact wording of the note to be sent out to America, Russia and Britain's European allies.

Eventually a wording was agreed on and the note was sent out; it was timed to arrive at its various destinations just as the Prime Minister rose in the House of Commons to give his second history-making speech in two days. The note read as follows:

Further to its recent decision on unilateral nuclear disarmament Her Majesty's Government proposes to take additional courses of action. To ask the North Atlantic Treaty Organisation (NATO) to declare the following:

a) an end to its policy of first-use nuclear weapons in a European war;

b) the withdrawal of all battlefield nuclear weapons from Europe; and

c) the withdrawal of all nuclear weapons targeted on Europe.

Unless these measures are carried out within three years of the date of receipt of this note then Her Majesty's Government will give notice to leave the North Atlantic Treaty Organisation.

Her Majesty's Government asks the United States Government to withdraw all its nuclear weapons at present situated in the United Kingdom *immediately* and in the event of the United Kingdom leaving NATO asks the United States to close down all its bases in the United Kingdom.

Her Majesty's Government is convinced that the years of friendship forged between our two countries will continue to exist and is sure that the United States will understand the reasons for our actions.

The United Kingdom calls upon the Soviet Union to give an assurance that once the measures outlined in this note are carried out no area of Western Europe will any longer be considered a target for nuclear attack by the Soviet Union.

Finally the United Kingdom asks all recipients of this note to agree to call an international conference to work out measures for worldwide multilateral nuclear disarmament.

The Reaction in Moscow

At the Kremlin, Moscow a meeting of the Political Bureau of the Central Committee of the Communist Party of the Soviet Union was about to begin. First Secretary Zinoviev reached for yet another cigarette as the last member of the twenty-man Politburo took his seat. Through a haze of smoke he peered down the table as the most important people in Russia read their copies of the British note.

There was silence as each one finished reading the note and raised their eyes towards Zinoviev; without saying a word their eyes showed their disbelief and amazement.

'You are going to ask me what we should do,' said Zinoviev.

'Well, comrades; we applaud their actions; we give them an immediate assurance that of course they will cease to be a nuclear target. We do everything in our power to make sure they carry out the measures in that note and after that we sit back and wait.'

'Should we not do something more positive than that? Perhaps we could point out strongly to the Americans that we support the British action.'

'No — no,' said Zinoviev, the ash from his cigarette dropping down on the table in front of him, 'you know the rules. Remember that Britain is an American satellite State; they have a free hand there just as we have a free hand in Eastern Europe. We must not provoke the Americans. We must let them act first. If they do nothing the Western capitalist alliance system will crumble; if they do act against Britain in any way they will be seen for what they are, a gang of dangerous bullies.

'No, comrades, we stand to gain most by doing nothing — at least for the time being.'

The Reaction in Washington

At the Oval Office of the President of the United States of America, Washington DC, Jerry Baines, newly elected President, sat in his swivel chair. He knew he faced the biggest test of America's power and prestige since the Cuban Missile Crisis way back in '62.

The members of his National Security Council sat around him.

'First thing, gentlemen, does this guy mean it; is this for real or some kind of stunt for domestic consumption or what?'

'Mr President, he means it.' It was Harry Bloomfield the President's security adviser and the only man to have met the new British Prime Minister. 'I think we have to accept that we are dealing with a sincere and possibly stubborn man; no matter how wrong-headed we believe him to be.'

'OK,' said Baines, 'what options do we have to sort out this one?'

'The first option, Mr President, is to do nothing and carry out the demands in the British note.' It was Bloomfield again.

'Or,' said Baines, 'do nothing full-stop and leave this guy to sweat it out.'

'Mr President, we in the Joint Chiefs of Staff believe you have to do something — you cannot do nothing nor can you withdraw our nuclear weapons from Britain.'

'Carry on, General,' said Baines, 'tell me more.'

'Mr President, you know the importance of Britain for American interests in the world, political and economic and military. We have fought two world wars to prevent Britain or Western Europe being dominated by any one country. We cannot stand by and allow our interests to take this knock because the Russians are going to dominate over there and if they do that we are in big trouble, Mr President, worldwide big trouble.'

'Also, Mr President, we have to think not just of the military consequences,' said Bloomfield, 'but also the political effects. If we do nothing what will happen to the strength of NATO? It will crumble, the Germans will run to do a deal with the Soviets; the French will seize the opportunity to call the tune in Europe. Remember what happened when the man who used to sit behind that desk did nothing about the Communists in Cuba; we nearly took the big plunge into war then. Mr President, we must act or the whole show will fold; the Russians will laugh their heads off and run riot round the world.'

'Let's see if we can run down the choice ladder gentlemen,' said Jerry Baines. One; we do nothing. Two; we obey the British demands. Three; we put pressure on the British to get them to reverse their decision — we have enough political and economic muscle to wreck the British economy, particularly if we can get the Germans and the Japanese to go along with us. This Prime Minister isn't made of steel, we can break him down if we want. We have enough friends in Britain to bring internal political pressure on him — OK so far?'

They all nodded in agreement.

'Four; we could go along with their call for nuclear disarmament. Anything else?'

'Mr President, in view of the British demand to withdraw our nuclear weapons *immediately* what you have suggested won't work; all the options you have come up with need time to work and if the British mean what they say then we can't have time. We need instant and effective action to deal with the situation.'

'What are you suggesting, General?' asked Baines.

'Direct military action, sir. It's the only way to nip this problem in the bud. I'd bet it's what the Russians would expect us to do;

it's the only way to keep our power and prestige in one whole piece.'

'You are suggesting a military invasion of a friendly, allied State, General?'

'If they are serious about the contents of that note Mr President they have ceased as of now to be a friendly, allied State.'

No one else spoke; Baines bit his fingernails; swivelled round in his chair and said, 'Very well, gentlemen, I want you all to go away now and put down in writing the options we have talked about and perhaps some more we haven't dreamed up yet. Tomorrow morning I want all those options on this desk and then I will decide; thank you.' Baines got up and left the room.

Jerry Baines did not get much sleep that night as he weighed the options in his mind. Early next morning he had a direct telephone conversation with the British Prime Minister; they spoke for half-an-hour. The Prime Minister would not shift one inch; Bloomfield had been right, the guy was really stubborn.

On the way along the corridor which led to the Oval Office he paused, thought for a moment; and then decided.

On his desk in the Oval Office lay the slips of paper with the options written clearly on them; each had a heading:

Do nothing.
Go along with the British demands.
Call an international disarmament conference.
Exert long term political and economic pressure on the British.
Military occupation of the British Isles.
And a new one which said, send a tough warning to the Russians not to interfere and reassure the Germans and other allies that the matter will be dealt with.

He shuffled the pieces of paper around; selected his choice, lifted the telephone, rang a number and spoke quietly, but firmly.

He finished, replaced the telephone on its hook and looked out at the bright spring sky over Washington DC . . .

(All characters are fictional; the events possible.)

TASKS: Chapter 18

1. Re-read 'Scenario for the Future'. You are Jerry Baines, President of the United States; what would you have done? And why?

2. You are the Prime Minister of Britain. Your American allies have deserted you; Russian tank armies are rolling across France, soon they will reach the Channel ports; an invasion seems likely; your own army has been wiped out; no one has yet used nuclear weapons.

   Call a Cabinet meeting and discuss the following choices:

   a)   surrender;
   b)   nuclear strike against Russian forces in France;
   c)   choice (b) plus destruction of Moscow;
   d)   no use of nuclear weapons — prepare for invasion with passive resistance and/or guerrilla warfare;
   e)   offer to install a Communist government if the Russians do not invade; or
   f)   negotiate a ceasefire.

   Which one do you choose? And why? Are there any other choices?

3. You are British Foreign Secretary; the Soviet ambassador has called to see you to object to Britain's possession of Trident missiles. Convince him or her that Trident is purely a deterrent weapon and not part of a NATO plan to strike first at the Soviet Union.

19 The effects of a nuclear attack on Britain

Councillor George Crabtree had been chosen to go to the meeting to represent his local council. His council, along with all others in Britain, is responsible for planning for emergencies at local level, whether they be floods, fires or earthquakes and so on.

The meeting Crabtree was to attend was to be about planning to deal with the results of a nuclear attack on Britain. He had been sent a whole wad of papers about the meeting. He had little chance to read them properly as he was too busy at work all day and about his council business most evenings.

Councillor Crabtree was in a good mood; he had just seen the dream of a lifetime come true; a new leisure centre for his town. It was his pride and joy; its main meeting room was called 'The Crabtree Assembly Room', which made him doubly proud. The young people of his town now had somewhere to go in the evenings; no excuses for vandalism now!

He did not drive directly to the meeting but stopped off at his local travel agent's to put down a deposit for his annual holiday; he and his family were going to Majorca in the summer.

When he arrived at the meeting he was surprised to find a group of people gathered round the entrance to the building holding banners and placards which announced such things as 'Ban the bomb'; 'No Cruise: No Trident'. There was even one which said 'Yanks Go Home'. Most of them had the symbol of the Campaign for Nuclear Disarmament on them.

Crabtree entered the building and was directed to a large hall; a man in army uniform was already talking to the audience. 'You can see from the map the sort of nuclear attack we can expect,' said the officer using a long stick to point at the map.

Crabtree found a seat at the back of the hall and stared up at the screen in front of him that showed a large map of Britain.

The officer went on, 'American bases are the first targets, particularly those which house cruise missiles. After these we can expect hits against London, Birmingham, Sheffield, Liverpool, Glasgow, Swansea, Bradford, Nottingham, Derby, Leicester . . .'

Crabtree did not need the voice to tell him, a glance at the map was enough; 'not a lot left' he thought as every major town and city in Britain seemed to have gone.

'We expect 125 nuclear bombs, the officer's voice droned on, 'with a total yield or power of 200 megatons. Most people within 5 miles of the centre of these explosions will be killed instantly. Of the 55 million people in the United Kingdom we expect around 30 million to be dead within minutes. This, however, we would describe as a moderate attack.'

Thirty million dead, 125 nuclear bombs, 200 megatons, thought Crabtree. He could not understand what that meant; the figures were just too large. He could only think of death in terms of himself, his family, his friends and neighbours. He stared at the map and for the first time saw that his own town was marked down for destruction. He could not think why anyone would want to destroy it. Crabtree saw in an instant the scene of death and destruction in his own

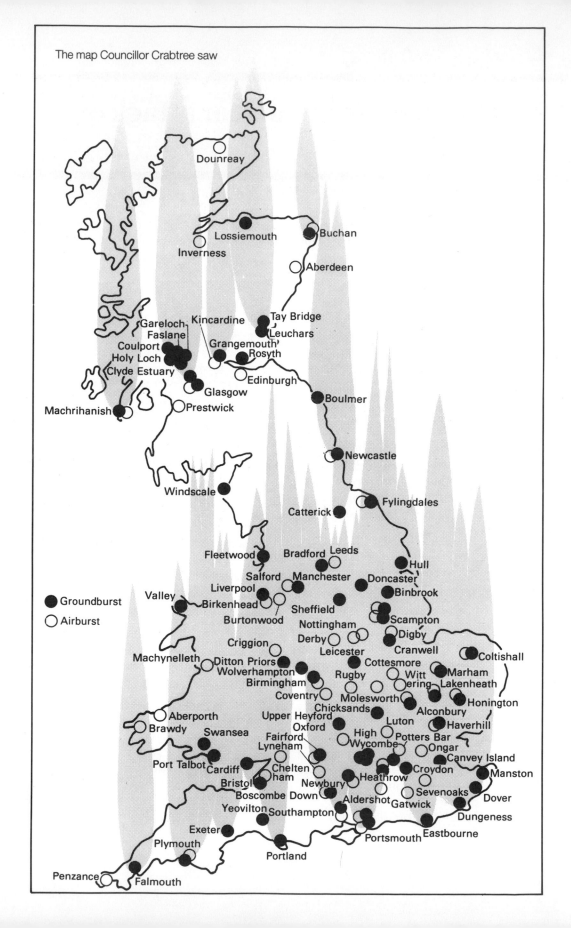

The map Councillor Crabtree saw

town; he realised he would die along with his family and everyone else.

'And so ladies and gentlemen we turn to the question of the survivors. They must avoid radioactive fallout which means they must stay at home; they must not attempt to move away. Home is the safest place which can be made even safer by the construction of a shelter against radioactive fallout. The survivors must stockpile food, water and medical supplies to last for at least fourteen days. To go outside before then would be to ask for death from radiation sickness.

'As we have no plans which provide for public fallout shelters or mass evacuation I repeat again our message: Stay put, stay at home; it's the safest place.

'Medical treatment will only be given to those likely to recover.

'Another problem that we will face, ladies and gentlemen, concerns those who refuse to obey our instruction to stay at home. The forces of law and order will not operate in a normal peacetime way because we will be faced with the greatest emergency situation of all time. The tasks of the police and army will be these:

'Maintenance of law and order, which will mean stopping refugees fleeing from our towns and cities; preventing looting; guarding food and medical convoys and stores. Naturally we will have to round up anyone who we believe could be of assistance to the other side and put them in camps. Special courts will be set up to deal with any offenders and because of the exceptional circumstances that will prevail after a nuclear attack special sentences will be carried out. It will be the duty of the police and the army to carry out these sentences.'

The man sitting next to Crabtree stood up and interrupted the officer and asked whether 'special sentences' meant that people who disobeyed might be shot?

'Yes,' said the officer.

This caused a murmur to ripple round the audience. The officer went on, 'You must remember that people will be in a state of shock or panic. If we are going to have an ordered society after a nuclear attack we must act quickly and firmly against those who threaten this.'

A woman at the front of the hall got up and asked, 'Just who will be controlling all these things?'

The officer replied, 'The United Kingdom will be divided into twelve regions; nine in England and one each in Scotland, Wales and Northern Ireland. Each region will be governed by a Regional Commissioner. The Regional Commissioner will have full powers until normal conditions return.'

'Normal,' thought Crabtree, 'could anything be normal after a nuclear attack?'

'Members of the Government and the armed services' chiefs and their staffs will be specially protected and have their own secret headquarters, so that they can take over from the regional commissioners as soon as possible.'

A lady spoke out behind Crabtree, 'What I find most disturbing is the lack of any proper civilian shelter programme: for instance there is one in both Switzerland and Sweden. Why don't we have one here?'

The officer replied, 'You must understand that neither Sweden nor Switzerland expect to be direct targets in a nuclear war so they can expect to save most of their people by providing shelters against radioactive fallout. We, on the other hand, expect to be a direct target; to protect against radioactive fallout would not save the millions who would die instantly and besides the cost of shelters for a country the size of our own would be huge. The Government believes that to follow the instructions given in the pamphlet *Protect and Survive* offers the best hope of surviving the effects of fallout.

'But most important of all you know we are protecting Britain and its people through our policy of deterrence. Now if we start to build public shelters for everyone in Britain that would give a clear signal to the enemy that we had abandoned deterrence and that we meant to attack him secure in the knowledge that our own people were protected.'

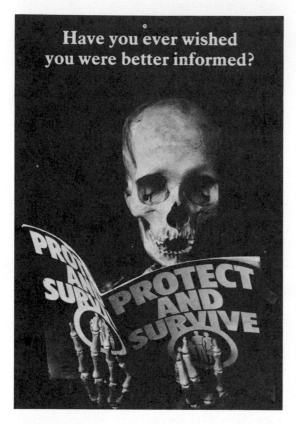

Have you ever wished you were better informed?

PROTECT AND SURVIVE

Crabtree fumbled in his pocket for his handkerchief, the room was hot and getting hotter. 'Stay put at home,' the man had said. Crabtree was beginning to wish that is what he had done; his new leisure centre no longer seemed the most important thing in the world.

After the meeting ended he hurried outside to his car and noticed that the demonstrators who had been at the door when he came in had now gathered in the field next to the car park. As Crabtree got into his car and started the engine he could hear the voice of the man who was addressing the crowd ringing loud and clear across the field.

'The Government's civil defence policy is nonsense. On the one hand we know that in the event of war, nuclear bombs will fall on or near every one of our towns and cities.

'And on the other hand we are told that people who live in these same areas must not leave them; in other words the policy is simply to stay put and die.'

Crabtree turned off his car engine and listened as the speaker went on,

'Is it likely that the population in our towns and cities will sit back and quietly accept this? I don't think so!

'I believe that people would take no notice of the Government's advice which would result in a mass flight from the towns into the countryside; even though the countryside would itself be contaminated by radioactive fallout.

'What would happen then? I'll tell you; roads out of target areas will be jammed with refugees. Already the Government has plans for closing all main roads against all but official vehicles. But what will happen when the crowds of refugees meet the police and soldiers who will refuse to allow them to use the roads? And what will happen to local councils in the countryside when they try to keep refugees out? For there will be no shelter and no food for refugees in the areas to which they go. The Government refuses to give enough funds to deal with this problem.

'How does the Government propose to deal with all this? I tell you the Government intends to rely on force to prevent refugees fleeing from our cities.

'All of this really cannot be described as civil defence; it defends no one except the privileged few who will occupy the bunkers at the outbreak of war. The mixture of lies and contradiction that makes up civil defence policy almost defies belief. But of course, this is inevitable, because the Government is attempting the impossible. It is trying to persuade us that we can survive a nuclear war.

'The only sane and practical solution to our civil defence problem is to remove all reason for a nuclear attack on this country.'

The rain which had been threatening to fall for some time now burst down on the field. Crabtree started his car engine, drove away and headed home.
(Sources: Government Civil Defence Exercise 'Square Leg' 1980 and CND.)

Britain is a small overcrowded island; 90 per cent of its people live in towns and cities; any nuclear attack on us would be an enormous disaster both in the short term and in the long term.

According to the British Medical Association Board of Science and Educational Inquiry into the Medical Effects of Nuclear War, 1983, a nuclear attack on this country might amount to anywhere between 15 to 200 megatons; the Government estimate is 200 megatons. However, a nuclear attack could be around 600 megatons because this is the amount needed to destroy cruise missile launching areas. These launching areas could be anywhere within 100 miles from their bases at Greenham Common in Berkshire and Molesworth in Cambridgeshire because the Government has said that cruise missiles will be dispersed up to these distances in times of crisis. As the Russians could not afford to allow cruise missiles to be fired at them because they are supposed to be unstoppable then they would have to destroy all possible launching areas within 100 miles radius of the cruise bases. This would require 600 megatons of explosive; three times the amount the Government estimates would fall on Britain.

As we have seen, nuclear weapons kill and contaminate by heat, blast and radiation. The results of these things on Britain would be as follows:

The destruction of food distribution services, and safe drinking water, fuel and power supplies would mean the spread of diseases. There would be no treatment for radiation sickness. As stated in the BMA report, 'Pain relief is likely to be grossly inadequate.'

In a nuclear war many people would be vapourised, but many bodies would remain as 'a continual reminder to the survivors of the horror they were experiencing.' Disposal of rotting corpses would be a major problem; for example after World War II it took the American army 8 weeks to bury 39 000 bodies. There might be millions of decaying bodies after a nuclear war.

A full scale attack on this country could mean 38.6 million dead and 4.3 million casualties immediately. The full horror is summed up by the BMA report:

'By the time the radiation hazard had fallen to acceptable levels for rescue (14–21 days), most of the seriously injured would have died from infection, radiation sickness, dehydration, exposure and shock.'

Food stocks within 6–12 miles of an explosion would be exposed to contamination by radioactive fallout. Farm animals are sensitive to radiation, but insects and vermin are much more resistant; flies, cockroaches and rats could survive and spread disease.

The Ministry of Defence told the British Medical Association that while some remote areas of Scotland and Wales would be safe from direct attack, 'there are very few areas of the United Kingdom that do not have some defence basing'.

TASKS: Chapter 19

1. *Preparations for Post-Nuclear Britain*
'The public has a right to knowledge of these matters.'
(Home Secretary, House of Commons 7/9/80.)

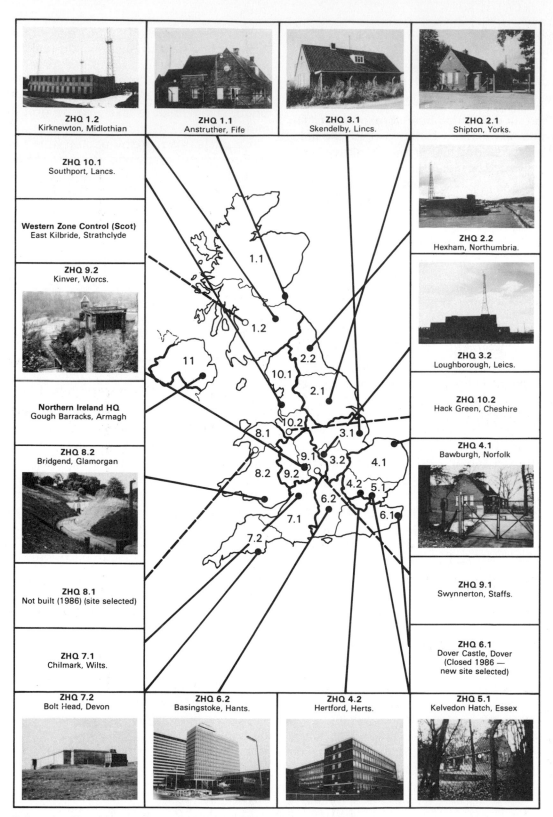

ZHQ 1.2
Kirknewton, Midlothian

ZHQ 1.1
Anstruther, Fife

ZHQ 3.1
Skendelby, Lincs.

ZHQ 2.1
Shipton, Yorks.

ZHQ 10.1
Southport, Lancs.

Western Zone Control (Scot)
East Kilbride, Strathclyde

ZHQ 9.2
Kinver, Worcs.

ZHQ 2.2
Hexham, Northumbria.

ZHQ 3.2
Loughborough, Leics.

Northern Ireland HQ
Gough Barracks, Armagh

ZHQ 10.2
Hack Green, Cheshire

ZHQ 8.2
Bridgend, Glamorgan

ZHQ 4.1
Bawburgh, Norfolk

ZHQ 8.1
Not built (1986) (site selected)

ZHQ 9.1
Swynnerton, Staffs.

ZHQ 7.1
Chilmark, Wilts.

ZHQ 6.1
Dover Castle, Dover
(Closed 1986 —
new site selected)

ZHQ 7.2
Bolt Head, Devon

ZHQ 6.2
Basingstoke, Hants.

ZHQ 4.2
Hertford, Herts.

ZHQ 5.1
Kelvedon Hatch, Essex

Sub-regional headquarters (bunkers) for controlling a post-nuclear Britain

Each county council in Britain has a 'war book' sometimes called a 'community survival guide'. These are kept at council offices at county and district level. They should also be in public record offices and main public libraries. Annual reports by police, water, fire and health authorities should contain details of their involvement in post-nuclear Britain.

Find out what you can about how your own area would be organised in post-nuclear Britain, and do not hesitate to quote the Home Secretary if needs be!

2. *Nuclear Free Zones — Resolution Passed by Manchester City Council*

> This Council, in the light of its pre-determined policy concerning the dangers of nuclear weapons, calls upon Her Majesty's Government to refrain from the manufacture or positioning of any nuclear weapons of any kind within the boundaries of our city.
>
> Conscious of the magnitude of the destructive capacity of modern nuclear weapons, we recognise that our proposals have little meaning on their own. We therefore directly appeal to our neighbouring authorities in the North West of England and to all local authorities throughout Great Britain to make similar statements on behalf of the citizens they represent.
>
> We believe that it is not in the interests of our people to be either the initiators or the magnet of a nuclear holocaust and firmly believe that such unequivocal statements would clearly indicate the overwhelming desires of the people we represent and could lay the ground-work for the creation and development of a nuclear-free zone in Europe.

Is this a practical proposition? What purpose do you think it serves? Can it be a first step to the removal of nuclear weapons from Britain? Or is it just wishful thinking?

3. *Civil Defence in Britain — Two Views*
   a) *Government advice*
      Read the Home Office pamphlet *Protect and Survive* which is meant to tell you how to improve your chances of survival; stay at home during nuclear attack; do not try to move around.
   b) *Campaign for Nuclear Disarmament — CND*
      The above advice is wrong and it won't work; the best course for Britain is to remove all reason for a nuclear attack through unilateral nuclear disarmament plus removal of American nuclear weapons.

Which of these views is more sensible? Give reasons for your choice. Would we be a nuclear target whether or not we had nuclear weapons or American bases because of our geographical position?

4. Cruise missiles would be dispersed up to 100 miles from their bases in the event of international tension: Cruise is based at Greenham Common near Newbury in Berkshire and will be deployed at Molesworth in Cambridgeshire. Locate these bases on a map and draw a circle to cover the dispersal areas. Do you live within either of them? Or know anyone who does? These are areas of certain and total destruction in the event of a nuclear war.

20   The way things could go

'Atomic weapons have changed everything except the way people think.'
(Albert Einstein)

The future of every man, woman and child on this earth lies in the hands of the leaders of the United States and the Soviet Union; they have the power to kill us all; they have the rivalry which might cause that power to kill us all.

What choices for the future do these people have? What will they do? What can they do?

Options for the USA *or* USSR

1.   *Unilateral disarmament* of all weapons, both nuclear and conventional, together with a refusal to settle any dispute by violent means. This choice can be called pacifist. Pacifism has a long history from early Christian teachings to the non-violent resistance used by Gandhi and his followers in India during the 1930s and 1940s. It can be expressed as follows:

> We utterly deny all outward wars and strife and fightings with outward weapons, for any end or under any pretence whatever; this is our testimony to the world ... the Spirit of Christ, which leads us into all truth, will never move us to fight and war against any man, with outward weapons, neither for the kingdom of Christ, nor for the kingdoms of the world.
> (Source: the manifesto of the Society of Friends of King Charles the Second of England, 1660.)

2.   *Unilateral nuclear disarmament* with strong conventional defence forces replacing nuclear weapons.
3.   *Unilateral nuclear disarmament* to be followed by a return to nuclear weapons if the other side does not quickly follow your example.
4.   *Multilateral nuclear disarmament* led by the Americans and Russians with other nuclear States 'persuaded' to follow their example.
5.   *Minimum nuclear deterrence*; keeping only *sufficient* nuclear weapons to deter an enemy attack.
6.   *Accept the nuclear arms race*; not much can be done to stop the arms race because it is in the nature of things; rivalry and aggression will always exist because that is the way people are. However, no attempt will be made to win the arms race, just enough will be done to keep pace with the other side.
7.   *Credible first strike*; gain the ability to start, fight and win a nuclear war; the threat of credible first strike can then be used to force concessions from the other side. This option means that not only must the arms race go on, but one side must achieve a significant lead over the other.
8.   *Concert of powers*; an old idea by which big powers club together to keep down the smaller ones or the ones who, in the future, might threaten them. America and Russia might say, 'There's plenty for both of us in the world; let's not fight, but concentrate on running the world together.' They might agree that Europe, China and perhaps Japan or India have to be kept under control before

they pose a threat to a world dominated by America and Russia.

9. *World democracy (American option only)*
The United States decides to destroy Communism in the world by encouraging subversion in Russia and China; surrounding them with military bases and forcing them to wreck their economies by ever-increasing arms expenditure. America could expect to win, especially if Europe and Japan go along with the idea. End result: a world dominated by the United States of America.

10. *World revolution (Russian option only)*
The Soviet Union decides to destroy the so-called democratic countries by encouraging subversion in America and Western Europe; surrounding them with military bases and forcing them to wreck their economies by ever-increasing arms expenditure. Russia could expect to win, especially if China goes along with the idea. End result: a world dominated by the Union of Soviet Socialist Republics.

11. *Preventive war*; one side uses its ability to strike first because it wants to prevent the risk of an *all-out* nuclear war; the only way to end the fear of nuclear devastation is to destroy the source of that fear once and for all; by destroying the other side it saves the world and of course becomes the dominant power. The fear of nuclear worldwide devastation is banished for ever.

These choices can and do overlap; several can be followed at the same time. Some are extreme solutions: some unlikely at present; some are already in operation. No matter how unlikely some may seem they are nonetheless choices which could be made in the future.

Britain's Choices

These are more limited than those available to the Soviet Union and the United States because of Britain's relatively weak economic and military position.

1. *Stay as we are*; with independent control of our nuclear weapons; member of NATO, dependent on the strength of the United States to deter a Soviet attack; American bases in Britain.

2. *Stand alone*; keep our nuclear deterrent; send the Americans home; tell the Russians that any attack on Britain will be met with retaliation against their towns and cities.

3. *Unilateral disarmament with the Americans sent home*

   a) Britain renounces all weapons of war — goes pacifist,

   b) Britain gives up nuclear weapons for ever,

   c) Britain gives up nuclear weapons and relies on conventional defence to deter an enemy attack,

   d) Britain gives up nuclear weapons as an example for others to follow; if they do not we will possess them again and return to 'stay as we are' option.

4. *Britain does a deal with the Russians*; Britain tells the Soviet Union that it will never use nuclear weapons against Soviet territory provided the Soviet Union removes Britain from its list of nuclear targets; Britain takes no further part in NATO and sends the Americans home.

5. *A bomb for Europe*; Britain negotiates an agreement with the French, the Germans and the Italians to construct a European nuclear deterrent which would establish Europe as an equal with the Americans and Russians. A nuclear Europe need not fear the Soviet Union nor have to depend on American promises to defend it. Europe could adopt a minimum deterrent policy or

join the run to 'win' the arms race and acquire a first-strike capability. Europe might then try to re-establish the domination of the world it held in the nineteenth century.

TASKS: Chapter 20

1. You are either the President of the United States or the First Secretary of the Communist Party of the Soviet Union. Call a meeting of your advisers and go through the choices listed under 'Options for the USA *or* USSR'. Which one or combination of options would you choose?
2. A General Election has been called, the main issue is Britain and its nuclear weapons. Organise political parties that support some or all of the options listed under 'Britain's Choices'; refer back to Chapter 17 'Britain and the Bomb' for information to include in your campaign.

   The arguments used may break down into two main strands — 'unilateralist' and 'multilateralist'.

   Here are some points used by the unilateralists.

   a) Get rid of our weapons and the American bases because:
      i) they make us a certain target for nuclear attack;
      ii) other countries will follow our example and disarm as well;
      iii) we will not be left defenceless because we will adopt an alternative or conventional defence;
      iv) the money saved by scrapping Trident will provide money for other projects; and
      v) the American bases must go not only because they are a target for nuclear attack but also because of our lack of control over them; in reality cruise missiles and other American weaponry are in the sole charge of the Americans.

   b) The British independent deterrent is not credible, the Russians do not believe we would ever use it.

   Here are some points used by the multilateralists.

   a) It is absolutely necessary to retain American involvement in the defence of Britain through a policy of deterrence that has kept the peace in Europe since the end of World War II.

   b) Unilateral nuclear disarmament is a sign of weakness; a sign that we no longer want any major involvement in Europe or the rest of the world. Our independent nuclear deterrent must be retained as a last resort weapon against attack should all else fail; we must never leave ourselves defenceless.

These two arguments still leave three options totally untouched: (1) Britain does a deal with the Russians (2) A bomb for Europe, and (3) Stand alone.

Form groups to fight the General Election on some of these choices. Detail your election manifestos.

Decide the result of the election by voting. Ask each voter to justify his or her decision.

Perhaps there are only *two* choices: *disarmament,*

> The world now stands on the brink of the final abyss. Let us all resolve to take all possible practical steps to ensure that we do not through our own folly, go over the edge
> (Lord Louis Mountbatten, Strasbourg, May 1979.)

or *death,*

Our President has just announced
A nuclear rocket strike of
At least one thousand megatons

Has been launched by the enemy
Directly at our major cities.
This announcement will take
Two and a quarter minutes to make,
You therefore have a further
Eight and a quarter minutes
To comply with the shelter
Requirements published in the Civil
Defence Code — section Atomic Attack.
A specially shortened mass
Will be broadcast at the end
Of this announcement —
Protestant and Jewish services
Will begin simultaneously —
Select your wavelengths immediately
According to instruction.
In the Defence Code. Do not
Take well-beloved pets (including birds)
Into your shelter — they will consume
Fresh air. Leave the old and bed-
ridden, you can do nothing for them.
Remember to press the ceiling
Switch when everyone is in
The shelter. Set the radiation
Aerial, turn on the geiger barometer.
Turn off your television now.
Turn off your radio immediately
The Services end. At the same time
Secure explosion plugs in the ears
Of each member of your family. Take
Down your plasma flasks. Give your children

The pills marked one and two
In the C.D. green container, then put
Them to bed. Do not break
The inside airlock seals until
The radiation All Clear shows
(Watch for the cuckoo in your
perspex panel) or your District
Touring Doctor rings the bell.
If before this, your air becomes
Exhausted or if any of your family
Is critically injured, administer
The capsules marked 'Valley Forge'
(Red pocket in No. 1 Survival kit)
For painless death. (Catholics
Will have been instructed by their priests
What to do in this eventuality.)
This announcement is ending. Our President
Has already given orders for
Massive retaliation — it will be
Decisive. Some of us may die,
Remember, statistically
It is not likely to be you.
All flags are flying fully dressed
On Government buildings — the sun is
shining.
Death is the least we have to fear.
We are all in the hands of God,
Whatever happens happens by His Will.
Now go quickly to your shelter.
(Extract from poem by Peter Porter *Your Attention Please*.)

References

Books and Journals
Effects of nuclear weapons

The Effects of Nuclear War, Office of Technology Assessment, Congress of the United States, Croom Helm, 1980.
(standard work on the effects of nuclear war).
The Effects of Nuclear Weapons, S. Glasstone and P. J. Dolan, US Department of Defense, 1977.
Nuclear Weapons, Home Office, HMSO, 1980.
Nuclear Radiation in Warfare, J. Rotblat, Taylor and Francis, London, 1981.
British Medical Association Board of Science and Educational Inquiry into the Medical Effects of Nuclear War, 1983.
Crucible of Despair: the Effects of Nuclear War, A. Tucker and J. Gleisner, The Menard Press, 1982.
Summary of Findings of the Washington Conference, Oct. 31st to Nov. 1st 1983: Nuclear Winter, Scientists Against Nuclear Arms.
The Fate of the Earth, J. Schell, Picador, 1982.
US Strategic Bombing Survey: the Effects of the Atomic Bombs on Hiroshima and Nagasaki, US Govt. Printing Office, 1946.
Japan National Preparatory Committee: Proceedings, International Symposium on the Damage and After-effects of the Atomic Bombings of Hiroshima and Nagasaki, Pergamon, London, 1978.
Note: The standard work — *The Effects of Nuclear War* — is a very expensive book and very detailed. *Crucible of Despair* and *The Fate of the Earth* are very good on the effects of all-out nuclear war.

The development of nuclear weapons

Brighter Than 1000 Suns, R. Jungk, Penguin, 1960.
(the story of the atomic bomb).

Men Who Play God, N. Moss, Penguin, 1968.
(the story of the hydrogen bomb).
The Advisers, Oppenheimer, Teller and the Superbomb, H. York, Freeman, 1976.

Nuclear weaponry

SIPRI Yearbook, Stockholm International Peace Research Institute.
(annual publication giving details of weaponry, also arms control and disarmament information).
IISS: Military Balance, International Institute of Strategic Studies.
(various publications on weaponry).
Janes Weapon Sytsems and *Janes Fighting Ships.*
(encyclopaedias with details of all modern armaments).
Ministry of Defence Review.
(annual publication on British weaponry and policy).

Arms control and disarmament

World Military and Social Expenditures, R. L. Sivard, WMSE, 1983.
(annual publication).
Arms Control and Disarmament Research Unit, Foreign and Commonwealth Office.
(pamphlets on arms control, disarmament and deterrence).
Arms Control and East–West Relations, P. Towle, Croom-Helm, 1983.

General works

As Lambs to the Slaughter, P. Rogers, M. Dando, and P. Van den Dungen, Arrow, 1981.
Nuclear Weapons: The Way Ahead, R. Gaskell; The Menard Press, London, 1981.

The Nuclear War Game, A. Suddaby, Longman, 1983.

Protest and Survive, E. P. Thompson, Campaign for Nuclear Disarmament and the Bertrand Russell Peace Foundation, 1980.

Speech on the Occasion of the Award of the Louise Weiss Foundation Prize to SIPRI, Lord Louis Mountbatten, Strasbourg, May 1979, Campaign for Nuclear Disarmament, c. 1980.

Nuclear Nightmares, N. Calder, Penguin, 1981.

The Third World War, General Sir John Hackett, Sphere Books, London, 1979.

Britain: civil defence and defence policy

Protect and Survive, Home Office, HMSO, 1981. (standard pamphlet giving advice for survival during and after a nuclear attack).

Domestic Nuclear Shelters, Home Office, HMSO, 1980.

Emergency Service 'ES' Circulars, Home Office. (official British planning documents for civil defence).

UK Warning and Monitoring Organisation, Home Office, HMSO, 1980. (document giving a brief description of how the organisation works, and would work, after a nuclear attack).

Civil Defence: the Cruellest Con-trick, Campaign for Nuclear Disarmament, 1979.

Target North-West, R. Poole and S. Wright, the Richardson Institute Study Group on Civil Defence, the Richardson Institute for Peace and Conflict Research, University of Lancaster, 1982. (deals with civil defence organisation and consequences of a nuclear attack on North-West England; although it is applicable to most parts of Britain).

The Defence of the Realm in the 1980s, D. Smith, Croom Helm, 1980.

The British Nuclear Deterrent, P. Malone, Croom Helm, 1984.

Defended to Death, G. Prins ed., Penguin, 1983. (most comprehensive work on unilateral nuclear disarmament).

Alternative Defence Policy, University of Bradford Peace Studies, Taylor and Francis, 1983.

The bomb and morality

Ethics and Nuclear Deterrence, G. Goodwin ed., Croom Helm, 1984.

The Church and the Bomb: Nuclear Weapons and the Christian Conscience, working party under the chairmanship of the Bishop of Salisbury, Hodder and Stoughton, 1982.

Films (16 mm)

Available from the British Film Institute Library, 81 Dean Street, London W1.

The Peace Game, Ministry of Defence, 1984. (pro-nuclear deterrent film).

Threads, BBC, 1984. (the effects of nuclear war).

Fail Safe, 1964. (dated but still gripping story of the consequences of early warning computer failure).

Dr Strangelove, 1963. (black comedy; details consequences of madness and nuclear war).

On the Beach, 1959. (life after a nuclear attack).

Available from Concord Films Council, 201 Felixstowe Road, Ipswich, Suffolk IP3 3BJ.

The Bomb, Yorkshire TV documentary.

The War Game, 1966. (now dated in many respects, but remains very real in impact as it portrays the horrors of nuclear war and its after-effects — also available from the BFI).

Some Addresses for Information on Nuclear Weapons

Home Office, F6 Division, Queen Anne's Gate, London SW1.

Foreign and Commonwealth Office, Arms Control and Disarmament Research Unit, Downing Street (East), London SW1 2AH.

Campaign for Nuclear Disarmament, 11 Goodwin Street, Finsbury Park, London, N4.

Pax Christi, Blackfriars Hall, Southampton Road, London NW5.

Quaker Peace and Service, Friends House, Euston Road, London, NW1.

World Disarmament Campaign, 238 Camden Road, London, NW1 9HE.

Scientists Against Nuclear Arms (SANA), 112 Newport Road, New Bradwell, Milton Keynes, MK13 OAA.

Further Work

The effects of nuclear explosions (physical, psychological and social) and civil defence provide the most substantial areas. However, any work in this area can lead to feelings of outrage and fear that nuclear weapons exist at all; which then provokes the question of what can be done to get rid of them. This leads to an investigation of the nuclear protest movement, its aims and methods. Any inquiry in this direction means a student will come across the political decision-making processes in Britain, the USA and USSR and beyond these the ideological, economic, social and political structures of these countries.

Peter Griffiths
1984

Nuclear weapons — Glossary

Airburst nuclear weapon — Weapon exploded in the earth's atmosphere below 100 000 feet.

Anti-Ballistic Missile (ABM) — Suggested development in the 1960s for a missile which could destroy an incoming enemy missile *before* it could reach its target. (see **Strategic Defense Initiative** for present-day equivalent).

Arms control — Talks or agreement between two or more countries to control armaments; can mean a *controlled increase* or *decrease* in weaponry.

Arms race — Name usually given to the attempts by the USA and the USSR to try to keep ahead of each other in the quantity and/or quality of nuclear weaponry.

Atomic bomb or **nuclear fission weapon** — The first kind of nuclear weapon; now regarded as a 'small'-yield weapon compared with the hydrogen bomb.

Ballistic missile — A missile aimed and fired like a bullet from a gun; totally unguided after launch. It depends for its effectiveness on the accuracy of the original aiming.

Ballistic Missile Early Warning System (BMEWS) — Line of radar stations covering North America giving the USA around fifteen minutes' warning of a missile attack.

Campaign for Nuclear Disarmament (CND) — British unilateral nuclear disarmament organisation.

Civil defence — Plans to protect people from the consequences of enemy attack.

Cold War — The state of mutual distrust which exists between the Western Alliance (NATO) and the Soviet Union and its allies (Warsaw Pact).

Collateral damage — Destruction of life and property in the core of a nuclear target area.

Command, Control and Communication (C3) — Military and political personnel and all the systems they use for communications; most easily damaged part of a nuclear weapons system.

Conventional weapons — All weapons that are not nuclear, chemical or biological.

Credible first-strike — Ability to convince an enemy that you can destroy that enemy's nuclear weapons by striking first.

Cruise missile — Now taken to mean a computer-guided, radar-evading missile.

Doomsday Machine — Originally an American idea to bury hydrogen bombs in the ground to deter a Soviet attack through the knowledge that such an attack would trigger the bombs and so destroy the world by splitting open the earth's crust.

Electromagnetic pulse (EMP) — A burst of electromagnetism resulting from a nuclear explosion which it is believed would black-out most communications systems over large parts of the earth.

Enhanced radiation weapon see **Neutron bomb**.

Fallout (radioactive) — Material sucked upwards by a groundburst nuclear weapon and then contaminated by dangerous radioactivity which returns to earth, sometimes many miles from the centre of the explosion; the effects of fallout can last for thousands of years.

First-strike — An attempt to destroy enemy nuclear weapons before they can be launched.

Fission — The splitting of atoms to release energy; usually refers to either uranium$_{235}$ or plutonium$_{239}$ used in atomic bombs.

Flexible response — Ability to use a variety of military responses to an attack as opposed to all-out, immediate use of nuclear weapons.

Fusion — Process used in the hydrogen bomb whereby materials join or fuse together to create a different substance; fusion releases massive amounts of energy.

Gamma rays — A penetrating form of electromagnetic radiation resulting from a nuclear explosion.

Groundburst nuclear weapon — Weapon exploded on or immediately above the ground.

Groundzero — Point on the ground at or immediately below the centre of a nuclear explosion.

Hotline — Telex link between Washington DC and Moscow to enable American and Soviet leaderships to communicate directly with each other in times of crisis.

Hydrogen bomb or **thermonuclear fusion weapon** — Standard nuclear weapon using an atomic bomb to trigger its explosion.

Intercontinental Ballistic Missile (ICBM) — Missile with a range of 3450 miles and over; capable of reaching North America when fired from the Soviet Union and vice versa.

Intermediate Range Ballistic Missile (IRBM) — Missile with a range of between 1726 and 3450 miles.

Killer-satellites — American idea for satellites in space to destroy, by laser or particle beam, enemy missiles after launch, but before they come near their targets. Sometimes known as battle-satellites or BATSATS.

Kiloton — Usual measure of the yield of atomic bombs; 1 kiloton equals 1000 tons of TNT equivalent explosive power.

Launch-on-warning — Because the warning times of missile attacks are so short it may become necessary to launch missiles as soon as radar systems pick up what 'could be' an attack.

Limited nuclear war — Suggestion that nuclear war can be limited to certain geographical areas without spreading to become all-out nuclear war.

Manoeuvrable Alternatively Targetable Re-entry Vehicle (MARV) — Missile carrying more than one warhead; these warheads can *alter* their courses to seek out many different targets after release from the missile carrying them.

Medium-Range Ballistic Missile — Missile within a range of 690 to 1726 miles.

Megaton — Usual measure of the yield of a hydrogen bomb; 1 megaton equals 1 000 000 tons of TNT equivalent explosive power.

Military – Industrial – Scientific – Complex (MISC) — Those people whose jobs and careers depend on continuing arms production.

Mini-nukes — Small-yield nuclear weapons, such as nuclear artillery shells.

Multilateral Disarmament — A process whereby many countries agree to a gradual and phased reduction in armaments; usually taken to mean any disarmament will be complete and total.

Multiple Independently Targetable Re-entry Vehicle (MIRV) — Missile carrying more than one warhead; these warheads can independently strike pre-determined targets.

Multiple Re-entry Vehicle (MRV) — Missile carrying more than one warhead; these warheads can be released separately over a target.

Mutually Assured Destruction (MAD) — The threat that if any enemy tries to destroy you then you will totally destroy that enemy in return.

Neutron bomb or **Enhanced radiation weapon** — Small-yield hydrogen bomb in which blast and heat outputs are decreased and radiation output increased; intended to kill people but leave property intact.

North American Aerospace Defense Command (NORAD) — American headquarters of warning system against Soviet attack.

North Atlantic Treaty Organisation (NATO) — Alliance of most Western European countries with the USA and Canada, formed in 1949 with the purpose of defending themselves against attack.

Nuclear delivery system — Aeroplanes and missiles which carry nuclear weapons.

Nuclear deterrence — Position whereby one country, successfully, *threatens* to use its nuclear weapons against another country if that country attacks it.

Nuclear fission weapon see **Atomic bomb**.

Nuclear freeze — American idea by which all research, production and placement of nuclear weapons would stop; intended to stop the arms race and so lead to nuclear disarmament.

Nuclear-free zone — An area where nuclear weapons are not manufactured, stored, deployed, or transported.

Nuclear proliferation — The spread of nuclear weapons and delivery systems to countries which do not already have them.

Nuclear weapon — Any weapon which uses the fission or fusion process to create an explosion.

Nuclear winter — Belief expressed by some scientists that the material sucked up by nuclear explosions will create a thick layer of cloud and so plunge the world into a harsh temporary winter; result could be extinction of all life on earth.

Plutonium$_{239}$ — Material that can be used in the manufacture of atomic or hydrogen bombs.

Prompt or initial radiation — Neutrons and gamma rays given out by nuclear explosions.

Protracted nuclear war — Idea that a nuclear war can be fought over days or months rather than over minutes or hours.

Rad — A measure of radiation received after contact with radioactive material.

Rem — A measure of radiation received which can be *harmful* to a living organism.

Short-Range Ballistic Missile (SRBM) — Missile with a range under 690 miles.

Strategic Defense Initiative (SDI) or **Star Wars** — American idea to stop an enemy nuclear missile attack before it can reach the USA. It involves the use of laser beams mounted on satellites high above the earth.

Strategic nuclear weapons — Those nuclear weapons that could be used to fight a nuclear war over long distances.

Submarine-Launched Ballistic Missile (SLBM) — Missile launched from a submarine; usually ICBMs.

Tactical nuclear weapons — Those nuclear weapons that could be used to fight a war over short distances.

Theatre nuclear weapons — those nuclear weapons intended for use in a war in one geographical area, e.g. Europe.

Thermonuclear fusion weapon see **Hydrogen bomb.**

Think-time — The time available between warning of a nuclear attack and the detonation of the incoming missiles.

Trident — Latest SLBM in use with the US Navy; being purchased by Britain for its submarine force.

Trinitrotoluene (TNT) — Conventional explosive used (a) as a trigger to a nuclear explosion and (b) as a measurement of nuclear explosion yields.

Unilateral nuclear disarmament — One-sided nuclear disarmament, one side gives up its nuclear weapons in the hope that others will follow its example.

Uranium$_{235}$ — Can be used as the explosive force in an atomic bomb.

Uranium$_{238}$ — Can be used as the explosive force in a hydrogen bomb.

Verification — Process whereby arms control and disarmament agreements can be monitored.

Warsaw Pact — An alliance between the Soviet Union and most Eastern Europe countries, formed in 1955 with the purpose of defending themselves against attack.

Yield — Name given to the explosive power of a nuclear weapon expressed in kilotons or megatons.

Index